DIFFUSIONS

Five Studies in Early History

To my wife

DIFFUSIONS

FIVE STUDIES IN EARLY HISTORY

BY

Gerald Bromhead Walker

THE RESEARCH PUBLISHING CO.
52 Lincoln's Inn Fields · London

ACKNOWLEDGEMENTS

The Author wishes to express his thanks to the authors and publishers as follows for their kind permission to quote extracts from their publications:

George Allen & Unwin Ltd, for permission to reproduce extracts from 'The Great Summons—Invocation to the Soul of a Dead Man' by Arthur Waley; *The Nine Songs* by Arthur Waley; *Seers, Shrines, and Sirens* by John Pollard; *Three Ways of Thought in Ancient China* by Arthur Waley. Thanks are also due to Barnes & Noble Inc. in respect of the latter work.

The University of Chicago Press for permission to reprint extracts from *Kingship and the Gods* by Henri Frankfort, Copyright 1948 by The University of Chicago. All rights reserved. Published 1948. Sixth Impression 1969. Printed in the United States of America. And from 'Symbol of a Symbol' by Angelo Brelich, and 'Indian Varieties of Art Ritual' by Miss Kramrisch, both from *Myths and Symbols,—Studies in Honour of Mircea Eliade.* Library of Congress Catalogue card number 69-12132. Copyright 1969 by the University of Chicago. All rights reserved. Published 1969. Mr Brelich's essay translated by Mr Nicholas Pogany.

The Clarendon Press for permission to make several quotations from *Kingship* by Hocart; also from *Greek Hero Cults and Ideas of Immortality* by Lewis Richard Farnell.

The Hamlyn Group for permission to reprint extracts from *Near Eastern Mythology* by John Gray; and from *Mexican and Central American Mythology* by Irene Nicholson. The latter work forms part of *The Mythology of the Americas.*

Harper & Row, Inc. for permission to reproduce passages from *Sumerian Mythology* by Samuel Noah Kramer.

The Cambridge University Press for permission to quote from *The Indian Theogony* by Sukmari Bhattacharji.

Routledge & Kegan Paul Ltd, for permission to reproduce a passage from *Classical Dictionary of Hindu Mythology* by John Dawson (Trubner's Oriental Series) and make quotations from *Cretan Cults and Festivals* by R. F. Willett. Acknowledgements in respect of the latter work are also due to the Humanities Press Inc.

Cassell and Company Ltd for permission to reprint a passage from *Deities and Dolphins* by Nelson Glueck. The U.S. & Canadian rights in respect of this book are controlled by Messrs Farrar, Straus & Giroux of New York, to whom thanks are due.

Columbia University Press for permission to reprint an extract from *Ancient Egyptian Religion* by Henri Frankfort, published by Harper & Row, New York, in Harper Torchbooks, 1961, pp. 8-14. (Originally published Columbia University Press, 1948).

Excerpts from *Thespis* by Theodore Gaster. Copyright 1950, 1961 by Theodore Gaster. Used by permission of Doubleday & Company Inc.

The British Museum for permission to reproduce a print of an Akkadian seal impression.

Printed in Gt Britain for The Research Publishing Co.
(Fudge & Co. Ltd), London

Contents

Illustrations

RITUAL OVERTONES IN
THE GRAIL LEGEND

The serious scholar must bear in mind that the world he is
exploring is infinitely different from the one he is familiar
with, and that his knowledge of it, however considerable,
must always be limited; that his experience of life is usually
immature, based as it is on the observation of a brief interval
of time, while the material at his disposal is a heap of isolated
ruins and fragments which often, seen from a single angle,
seem inauthentic, but later, when transposed into their
true context, belie such premature judgment.

J. J. Bachofen

The castle they said could not be found.
Familiar Blurb.

INTRODUCTORY

At the time when Miss Jessie Weston published her first study of the Grail legend, the fertility aspects of early religious observances were receiving particular attention. Treated basically by the methods of comparative anthropology, these tended to overshadow the effects on religion of great historical movements, and the closer association of religion with State. Moreover, the principle having been accepted that, among primitive peoples, religion was and is a concern of the tribe or community, the position of the individual tended to be overlooked.

In the sphere of anthropological studies, as in the contemporary religious and political environs, it is necessary constantly to widen the field of study—and indeed action—to its true and abiding dimensions. On the broader scale, the significance of Power, overshadowing even the forces of nature, must not be forgotten: in the narrower and humanistic aspect, the importance of the individual to himself should, on every sound psychological ground, have the first and last word.

Man's relationship with the worldly power that nurtures and protects him is an ever-present political problem. His relationship with his spiritual 'authorities' is equally fluid. No man is a spiritual island in space. Equally, no savage is free, even in his conceptions of an after-life. But continuance, if only in his position within the tribe, is ensured, so far as tribal rituals are able to facilitate this.

The mystique of the Grail ought therefore to be considered as one aspect of ancient cultures in their totality, rather than as a particular cult that was captured by a particular dogma. Our initial casts must be very wide, and reach a very long way back in time.

A cursory examination of what we know of human history will suggest that fertility rites and cults have represented only a single, though recurring, theme in the drama of human aspiration. Our earliest—pictorial—records are of a hunting culture. General fertility practices are not evident in paleolithic cave art, possibly because the hunter was not interested in proliferating beasts of prey and noxious insects and reptiles, despite his respect and even admiration for the animal kingdom. He certainly sought allies and guardians within that kingdom, hence probably the beginnings of Totemism. He, or rather his tribe, may have looked for rebirth within a favoured animal species. He executed his animal paintings in the remotest accessible depths of his cave, and this suggests that he wished them to be preserved in the safest possible place, within reach of the fount of creation in the bowels of the earth, and that he already conceived of them as his own, or his tribal, external or alternative soul.

Featured among these paintings is a human figure in a composite animal disguise. This is clearly a Shaman. This figure links the Magdalenian culture with contemporary cultures widely dispersed throughout the remoter parts of the earth. The institution of Shamanism has been fully examined by Mr Mircea Eliade. The Shaman is, and was, far more than a mere medicine man. His initiation, by an older and established Shaman, is long and arduous, and involves an act of ritual death and revitalisation. He is frequently selected for the office against his own wishes. His office is not sought after, which illustrates a point well made by Mr Eliade. Few people have ever wished to be elected, or to dedicate themselves, to the devotional life, or to assume the lonely mantle of the prophet. Throughout history there has been a tendency to concentrate all the

rigours and responsibilities of religion on a few reluctant
individuals, be they priests, kings, or merely youths or
animals distinctive for their physical perfection.

Broadly speaking, the Shaman fulfils two functions. He
advises on hunting, and he exercises pastoral care in sickness or death. In the former role, he identifies himself with
various animals, hence his disguise in the cave paintings.
Generally speaking, the wearing of 'travesties' and masks in
primitive life is an act of identification. In this capacity,
his earliest manifestations, he was the prototype of the
'Lord of the Animals'. Since, in our age at least, a Shaman
can be a woman, such was probably the original 'Lady of
the Animals'. This title developed into an attribute of godhead. Shiva is a notable 'Lord of the Animals', and is depicted as such in iconography of the Indus Valley civilisation.
Ariadne, the mother goddess of ancient Crete, is one instance of a 'Lady of the Animals'. The Shaman's latter
function, that of the pastoral care of his tribe in sickness
and death, is more relevant to our immediate subject.

There is no question but that the central thread of all
psychic and religious thought and practice, from the earliest
times, has been the protection of the individual human
personality in life, and its care in sickness and death. That
the individual, in primitive conditions, is regarded *au fond*
as an indissociable member of his tribe, does not in practice
invalidate this principle. The Shaman cares for an individual in sickness, usually by the expedient of securing or
calling back his soul, which is deemed to have fallen into
the power of a sorcerer or ghost, since death is not regarded by primitive peoples as a natural and inevitable
phenomenon. In practices which may have derived from
the theological concepts of early civilisations, the Shaman
guides a departing soul to its place in the underworld.
The magical formulae set forth in the Egyptian Book of the
Dead have the same object, though here it is cast in the

11

highly ritualistic and magical forms that we associate with Egyptian religion. The Tibetan Book of the Dead offers the same service in terms of Buddhist belief. As Mr Eliade makes plain, the Shaman utilises emotional aids to stimulate his higher imaginative or psychic flights. In modern parlance, he 'gets sent' with the help of song, drumming, and the dance. Like Shiva, he is 'Nataraj', or lord of the dance. He was probably the earliest poet. 'The Great Summons—Invocation to the Soul of a Dead Man', a Chinese poem translated by Mr Arthur Waley, illustrates, in highly literary style, the aspect of shamanistic procedure which involves the recalling of the wandering soul of a sick man.

> Oh Soul go not to the South
> Where mile on mile the earth is burnt away
> And poisonous serpents slither through the flames . . .
>
> Oh Soul go not to the West
> Where level wastes of sand stretch on and on:
>
> Oh Soul go not to the North,
> To the Lame Dragon's frozen peaks:
>
> Oh Soul go not to the East,
> To the silent Valley of Sunrise! . . .

The dangers which threatened at all times the individual, and potentially the tribe, are many and varied, and some more immediate than others. Death out hunting, or by murder or sorcery, would constitute the most immediate perils. The age of war introduced its own version of the Waste Land. What freak of climate could measure up with the deliberate scorched earth policy of dark age and Norman strategy in the British Isles? The period of heavy agriculture, and, stemming from it, that of the pastoral peoples of the limberlost, was also the age of War, an age which has been insufficiently studied by comparative anthropology.

If war, as the occasion of special beliefs and observations, has received inadequate attention in anthropological studies, the recognition of the major importance of kingship in the development of ritual systems has also been tardy. Many of the conclusions reached by Hocart in *Kingship* were probably premature, and have been reversed by subsequent research. Few anthropologists would now join him in attributing all belief in God and immortality, and all initiation ceremonies, to the institution of kingship, nor would they agree that the sacred king was *ab origine* identified with the sun. Frazer's ideas on the evolution of kingship from priesthood are still acceptable in principle. The origins of kingship as we know it are coeval with the beginnings of recorded history, and the earliest records in Egypt and Mesopotamia relate the king to the supreme god of the land, who was by no means at that time solely the embodiment of the powers of the sun.

That priesthood preceded kingship in terms of historical chronology is almost beyond argument, if the Shaman may be considered to have been the prototype of the priest.

In highly evolved communities, political considerations, particularly the need for a leader in war, have repeatedly compelled the re-establishment of a king. He was certainly the summation of all cults, public and personal. The well-being of the land in all its aspects was vested in him. But apart from this, and from the point of view of his subjects, he performed a function that is implicit neither in purely state sacral functions nor in the conditions of enemy attack; that is concerned neither in the health of the soil nor in the dangers of invasion. He was the mediator between the man and his gods, and relieved the individual of much of the burden of ritual service and of expiation. Thus in ancient Mesopotamia the king would be required to perform

prolonged and arduous penances under the direct super-
vision of his priests and astrologers, while the common man
could go about his business and indulge in his pleasures.
This function alone was sufficient to endear his subjects
to a rule which might, at other times, be autocratic and
burdensome. The king was the supreme mediator and scapegoat, and could be, as we shall see, man's principal link
with the hereafter.

In this study the writer makes no attempt to go beyond
the strict terms of the title. The novel, or romance, of the
Grail will probably never be reduceable to one grand ritual,
still less to one set of circumstances, historically identifiable. It certainly invokes ritual elements that the writer,
with the assistance of his sources, has clearly identified in
ancient Middle Eastern practice. Other elements, such as
those involving the even more ancient institution of Shamanism, are present in the story only as beliefs, or concepts,
although these too in their earliest forms were associated
with rituals. At all events it is hoped that this study will
serve to demonstrate that the character of the suffering
God cannot be reduced to the scale of a humble victim of
an obscure fertility ritual.

I

In the course of a long conversation with Trevrizent, the
hermit, Parzifal's uncle and brother to Amfortas, the former tells Parzifal that 'If anywhere a land loses its lord, if
the people there acknowledge the Hand of God and seek a
new lord, they are granted one from the company of the
Grail. They must treat him with courtesy, for the blessing
of God protects him.' (Wolfram von Eschenbach, Book IX).
The choice of a king in ancient times appears to have
been the prerogative sometimes of a sacred place, and

sometimes specifically of a God or a Goddess: but in the case of the sacred place, it may be assumed that what is meant is the priesthood resident in that place.

For instance, in Sumeria of the time of the first dynasty, the kingship was at the disposal of the holy city of Nippur. This circumstance has a special significance attached to it, since it seems that in the earliest times in Sumeria a King was only installed in times of emergency. The Babylonian goddess Ishtar is later credited with the same authority, but in early Mesopotamia in general it was the custom for the assembly of the cities to grant ascendency in the land from time to time to a specific city, and it was this city that disposed of the kingship.

In ancient Egypt, Isis is depicted graphically with the determinative of a throne on her head. Indeed, Henri Frankfort in his brilliant study *Kingship and the Gods* suggests that Isis was originally the deified or personalised throne. Her very name would imply this, but there is also a most suggestive incident that is related in that highly entertaining document known as the Chester Beatty Papyrus. In the course of the extensive law-suit that is entered into by Horus against Seth for the crown of Egypt, Isis, who has hitherto supported Horus her son in his claim, unexpectedly changes sides and attacks Horus, who has transformed himself into a hippopotamus, with a harpoon. Horus thereupon beheads her with a sixteen pound cleaver, and goes off with her head into the mountains, upon which Isis turns herself into a headless flint statue. Nothing could more clearly illustrate a temporary de-personalisation into the throne that is represented by the goddess.

Herakles was identified with a number of Palestinian deities, among them the Phoenician god Melqart in Tyre, and Samson in Philistia. Herodotus states that the earliest dynasty in Lydia claimed descent from Herakles. The tradition held that the first king of the dynasty was a son of Herakles by a slave girl or *hetaira* who was a daughter of Iardanos. It has been supposed that the identification of Herakles with the legendary ancestor of this race was a Greek interpolation, and that the actual tradition referred to a Hittite god, Sandan. The position of a *hetaira* as the mother of a dynasty in Asia Minor was illustrated by Bachofen, the nineteenth century Swiss philosopher, in his study of the Tanaquil tradition.

A statue of Tanaquil stood in Roman times in the temple of Dius Fidius beside the temple of Herakles. Tanaquil was an Asiatic goddess whose immediate provenance was Etruscan, and her significance for our argument lies in the tradition of the part she played in the conception of Servius Tullius. There was a slave girl or *hetaira* in the household of Tarquinius Priscus named Ocrisia. Whilst Ocrisia was about her sacrificial duties, a phallus reached out for her. Tanaquil, here represented as a living woman, witnessed this event, and, prophesying a superhuman ancestry for the girl, ordered her to put on bridal attire. In due course, she gave birth to Servius Tullius.

It is notable that Tarquinius Priscus and Tarquinius Superbus both attained the crown as the gift of a woman.

Bachofen traces the mystique of these traditions back through Etruscan and Sabine tradition to the Mylitta cult among the Sacaea of Babylonia.

Kundry is the agent who, at the end of Eschenbach's Parzifal, summons the hero to return to the Grail Castle and assume the sovereignty.

She thus relates to those goddesses, of which we have treated above, who exercised a right to select, or confirm, candidates for the kingship. There is an early, and fragmentary, Egyptian text which tells how Hathor conducted a wholesale massacre of the human race. The story is, in fact, a form of Flood myth, and its origins need not concern us further here.

A similar story is told of Anat, the sister of Baal in a Canaanite text:

> She slaughters the people of the coast lands,
> Annihilates the population of the east.
> At her feet [roll] heads like balls;
> Above her fly limbs like locusts.
> The limbs of the henchmen . . .
> She ties the heads around her bosom,
> Dangles the limbs from her girdle . . .
>
> (*Thespis* by Theodor Gaster)

Like an infernal Don Quixote, she proceeds to attack tables and chairs, under the impression that they are soldiers.

The fact has generally baffled commentators that early nature goddesses of Mesopotamia were also War Goddesses. The reason for this, it would seem, is that a goddess capable of destruction on the scale described would also be likely to make a successful general in battle.

No incidents of this kind are attributed to Kundry. However, her appearance is described in iconographic terms in Parzifal.

'She had a nose like a dog's, and two boars' teeth stuck out from her mouth, each a span in length. Both eyebrows were braided, and the braids drawn up to the ribbon that held her hair. She had ears like a bear's, and her face was hairy and rough. Her hands looked like a monkey's skin. Her fingernails stuck out like a lion's claws' (Book VI).

'Her eyes were yellow as topazes, her teeth were long, her mouth shone blue as violet' (Book XV).

We have here an excellent picture of Kali, the Indian goddess of life and death. In her creative aspect she is portrayed as a beautiful woman, in her destructive aspect she is depicted in the terms applied to Kundry, and in addition

she wears the lopped off limbs, the skulls, etc., appropriate
to Anat.

II

Tales of the miraculous birth of a king, or of the founder
of a dynasty, bring us to a wider field, that of the cult
of the Hero, who features in both legendary and historical,
or quasi-historical, circumstances.

The subject of the Hero, in its ritual aspects, has been
treated at length by Lord Raglan. In *The Hero*, Lord Raglan
draws up a notional summary of the outstanding episodes
in the life of a Hero, listed in chronological order. The
first half of his life, in which he assumes the kingship, is
defined in the following stages:

1. The hero's mother is a royal virgin;
2. His father is a king, and
3. Often a near relative of his mother, but
4. The circumstances of his conception are unusual, and
5. He is also reputed to be the son of a god.
6. At birth an attempt is made, usually by his father or his
   maternal grandfather, to kill him, but
7. He is spirited away, and
8. Reared by foster-parents in a far country.
9. We are told nothing of his childhood, but
10. On reaching manhood he returns or goes to his future
    kingdom.
11. After a victory over the king and/or a giant, dragon,
    or wild beast,
12. He marries a princess, often the daughter of his pre-
    decessor, and
13. Becomes king.

18

Lord Raglan then proceeds to illustrate this pattern with reference to the legends attaching to the lives of a number of traditional, and a few historic, characters. At this point we prefer to return to Egyptian sources.

The murder of Osiris, who henceforth assumes his classic role of the Dead King, was the work of Seth. The various texts that recount the story of the life and death of Osiris do not represent it as a ritual killing, a divine sacrifice. It is a murder, and the basic reason for it is that, as was mentioned above, death by natural causes was not in those days recognised. No one could just die, a divine king least of all. If a king died, he had to be killed, and he could only be killed by a God. Thus Seth, who was a God, one of the Ennead, played a part that later fell to the God of Death in many religious hierarchies. (He is in fact believed to have been in origin a pre-dynastic indigenous god.)

After the death of Osiris, Isis is magically impregnated by him, and bears Horus. She is imprisoned by Seth, but escapes from captivity and flees with her baby son into the marshes of the Delta. Seth attempts to poison Horus, but is frustrated by the good offices of Thoth. Soon after, she leaves Horus with friendly strangers and takes up the vocation of a beggar to support herself.

There is a long break in this, may we say, fated story, while the texts suggest that Seth ruled in Egypt. Then follows the return of Horus, and the law suits and ritual combats by which he regains the throne.

Egyptian religion was far too specialised and ritualised to bear transplantation except in certain specific respects. There is little evidence of even 'low level' intercourse between Egypt and Mesopotamia in Sumerian I dynastic times. There are marked differences between Egyptian and Mesopotamian concepts of kingship in respect of the relationship of the king to his gods. The Mesopotamian king was the servant of the gods, and a humble servant at

that, and only in a few cases claimed to be divine. As we
shall see, the Egyptian king was nothing if not divine.

Elements of the typical Hero-king birth legend we have
referred to appear in the biography of Sargon of Akkad,
the founder of the Agade dynasty, the Second Dynasty of
Ur. He was said to be the son of a priestess, and was set
afloat at birth in a reed cradle, and rescued and brought up
by a gardener. To move a long way forward in time, the
same story is told of Darab, one of the last kings of the
Persian Achamanean dynasty. His mother bore a child by
her father, Bahman, and when she came to the throne at
his death she disposed of the embarrassing infant by float-
ing it on the Euphrates. The tale, which is related in the
Shah-Namah, describes how the casket was followed by
two observers, to see that it should come to no harm. It
was found by a fuller, who brought the young prince up
until he was of age to assume the throne.

Assurbanipal II of Assyria addressed the following invocation to Ishtar:

> I was born among mountains which no one knew
> I did not recognise thy might and did not pray to thee.
> The Assyrians did not know of thy godhead and did not
>   pray to thee.
> But thou, O Ishtar, fearsome mistress of the gods,
> Thou didst single me out with the glance of thine eyes.
> Thou didst take me from among the mountains.
> Thou didst call me to be a shepherd of men.
> Thou didst grant me the sceptre of justice.
>   (Quoted from *Kingship and the Gods* by Frankfort).

These examples of the observance of extraordinary
birth and succession customs in historical dynasties are of
particular interest, since they shed light on the instances
quoted by Lord Raglan where they refer to legendary cult
heroes. These were Oedipus, Theseus, Romulus, Perseus,

Jason, Bellerephon, Pelops, Asclepios, Dionysus, Apollo, Zeus, Siegfried, Llew Llawgyffes, Robin Hood, and Arthur. We can, of course, add Parsifal to this list. The point is made by Frankfort that the object of these customs was to furnish proof that the king was placed on the throne by divine selection, even when he was not of royal descent, as in the case of Sargon of Akkad. In many instances, if examined in detail, we find that the chosen king was of royal descent, but that his claim could be disputed by relatives. But in many also, such as those we quoted earlier, the birth is represented as flatly divine, the engineering of a priest, god, or goddess. Instances recorded in literate times are doubtless vestigial, but cognate practices serve to illustrate that ritual evidence of divine selection, and in some cases actual evidence of identity were frequently required.

The episode of Arthur and the 'Sword in the Stone', for instance, recorded a ritual current in bronze and iron age times by which the heir to a throne was required to draw out a sword that had been driven into the barrow erected over the late king's grave.

Gawain in the Perlesvaus version is told that he 'may not enter the castle (that guards the entrance to the land of the Holy Grail) nor come nigher to the Holy Grail save you bring the sword wherewith St John was beheaded.' The reference to St John is a later Christian interpolation: elsewhere this sword is said to become bloody at noon, thus revealing it as a weapon borne by a knight or king under the aegis of the sun/war cult.

The significance of the form of words that Parsifal failed to put to the sick Grail king on his first visit to the Grail castle has baffled most commentators. He should have asked simply, 'What is the matter with you?' The precise text was probably more elaborate. The incident has, in fact, an exact parallel in that of Oedipus and the Sphinx, except that Oedipus answered the riddle correctly. There could be no risk that the true heir might not give the 'password' on presenting himself, and this was evidently a close family secret.

III

Parallels between the story of Parsifal and that of Kai Khusrau of ancient Persia have been noted by authorities, and treated at some length by Sir J. C. Coyajee, in his work *Iranian and Indian Analogues of the Legend of the Holy Grail,* published in Bombay by Taraporevala.

Kai Khusrau's grandfather is Kai Kaus. His father Siyawash has been slain by the Turanian king Afrasiyab, whose daughter is Kai Khusrau's mother. Afrasiyab lays waste the land of Iran, but fails to achieve the throne during the lifetime of the aged Kai Kaus. He is aware of the existence of Kai Khusrau, and wishes to put him to death, but is persuaded not to when Kai Khusrau is brought before him, and answers all his questions in idiotic fashion, thus convincing Afrasiyab that he is half-witted. Kai Khusrau is then sent away to be brought up by shepherds.

Parsifal is represented in his youth as ignorant, ill-mannered and bucolic, and fails to provide the requisite form of words on his first presentation at the Grail Castle. This is not surprising, because at the time there is another pretender to the crown, Parsifal's uncle, the Roi del Chastel Mortel, who is shown in the Perlesvaus version of the story as making war upon the Fisher King for possession of the royal emblems.

A further analogy between the stories of Parsifal and Kai Khusrau lie in the account of the test by which the latter finally establishes his claim to the throne. He demolishes the magic fort, Bahmandez, by means of a conjuration placed in the point of a lance, which is thrust into the gate. This, in the Arthurian legend, is the castle of Klingsor.

Only in the later, Christianised versions of the Grail story is the Holy Grail itself the object of the quest. The original purpose of the quest was to release the land from the curse under which it lay, or to heal the sick king. The Grail itself did not contribute directly to these ends.

Sir J. C. Coyajee believed that the Holy Grail was identical with the Royal Glory, the quest for which receives prominent mention in the Zend Avesta, particularly in the Astad Yast and Zamyad Yast.

It is described as 'the Aryan Glory, the awful Kingly Glory, rich in food, rich in flocks, rich in wealth'. It 'destroys Aeshma, the fiend of the wounding spear'. It is the 'glory that cannot be forcibly seized.' Whoever has it, 'Victory will cleave unto him' . . . he will 'conquer the havocing hordes.' It belongs to 'the bright ones' . . . 'it is they who shall restore the world, which will thenceforth never grow old and never die . . . when the dead will rise, when life and immortality will come.'

The Turanian 'murderer' or 'ruffian', Afrasiyab (see above) tried to seize the Royal Glory in the sea Vouru-Kasha, where it is described as waving, as though it were seaweed. 'He stripped himself naked, wishing to seize that Glory. . . . but the Glory escaped, the Glory fled away, the Glory changed its seat'.

As a result of his failure to capture the Royal Glory, Afrasiyab failed to achieve the throne of Iran, though he ruled for two hundred years over the Turanian kingdom, at the end of which time he was defeated by Kai Khusrau, and pursued by him to an underground palace of vast dimensions, with walls of iron and a hundred columns—a type of the Castle of the Otherworld, or Underworld.

The Kavaem Hvareno in Zend, or the Farr in old Persian, are both words which mean 'kingly light' or 'light'. A reference to the Royal Farr in the Shah-Nama makes its actual quality clearer. The legendary king Jamshid was succeeded by a Dragon King named Zahhak, who reigned a thousand years, and reduced Iran to idolatry and wickedness. Towards the end of his reign, a hero named Faridun was born. 'The Royal Farr radiated from him. It had been inherited from Jamshid, and he was as refulgent as the sun that shines in the heavens . . . '

Thus it was in fact a quality which conveniently fitted princes who succeeded or were elected to the throne; although its presence in certain episodes at the bottom of the sea points to a connection with the creation process to which we will refer later. A brilliant light was, of course, shed around the Grail in the legends.

Notable throughout legendary history is the association of a divine or familiar animal with certain monarchs. When Ardashir, who is to found the great Sassanian dynasty, is escaping from his master Ardavan, the last Parthian king of Iran, he is followed by a huge ram. Ardavan asks his counsellor the meaning of this phenomenon, and the latter replies 'It is his Farr. In his kingliness, through the blessedness of his star, it acts as his protection. If this ram keeps pace with him, pursue no further.'

A strange tale is told of Bahram, a general who usurped the throne of Iran. Before this event, he meets a wild ass (Onager) which guides him to a castle, where a follower sees him in conversation with a beautiful woman seated on a throne. He leaves the castle, weeping tears of blood, still guided by the Onager. His reign was short and troubled.

Samson, it would seem, was aided in his battles by the Farr of an Onager, the text having been corrupted in translation.

The association here recounted between the Royal Glory, a helpful animal, and a goddess is significant, since it is a horse which, as we will see, brings Gawain to the Grail, albeit against his will.

IV

The Coronation ceremony is fully described by A. M. Hocart in *Kingship*. There is also a chapter devoted to the custom of the preparation of a divine and royal drink that is taken in the course of the ceremony.

The classic ambrosia was the Soma of Ancient India. This was the food of Gods and Kings. The name means simply 'pressing', but the substance bore the alternate name Amrita, 'the immortal', since it was believed to confer immortality. The Persian equivalent was Haoma. This property of giving immortality, or at least prolonging life, belongs to the Grail.

The material used in the preparation of the drink itself has varied greatly, and may at times have been an intoxicant.

In Ancient India, the plants used were fictionalised as the Tree of Life, which had been transplanted to the mountains. This information we owe to a curious work entitled *The Ruling Races of Prehistoric Times* by J. F. Hewitt (Constable 1894). Regarding the Persian Haoma sacrifice, Hewitt refers to a reference contained in the Khorshed Myaris in the Zend Avesta.

> We sacrifice unto the golden instrument,
> We sacrifice unto Mount Saokanta, made by Mazda.

Hewitt quotes a Sanskrit commentator on this passage, but we have been unable to find the source of this gloss.

'On Mount Saokanta there is a golden tube coming from the root of the earth: the water that is in the surface of the earth goes up through the hole of that tube to the heavens, and being driven by the wind spreads everywhere, and thus the dew is produced.'

25

Mount Saokanta is the great central mountain of the world, which features in all Asian mythologies. The tube, according to Hewitt, is also symbolised by the stalk of the lotus.

In the Bleheris or Bilihis version of the Grail story, Gawain, while in the Hall of the Holy Grail, sees a lance, fixed upright in a silver cup, from the point of which flows a continuous stream of blood, which is carried by a spout of emerald into a golden tube, and so out of the hall. This detail is mentioned by Miss Jessie Weston in *The Quest of the Holy Grail*, page 35.

Hocart says, 'In order to prepare Soma they have first to crush it, but Soma is a god, and thus they crush a god and a king', and 'in pressing out a king they slay him'. 'King Soma' is thus conceived as a king that is immolated. But sin would be incurred by slaying a god, and therefore when they strike the Soma in crushing they say, "Herewith I strike So-and-So, not thee"; thus no guilt is incurred'.

Such ritual evasions of guilt are a commonplace of folklore. Writing still of the Vedic ritual, Hocart continues (page 213) 'Soma is bought from a eunuch because he is neither man nor woman, with lead because it is neither gold nor iron, with a liquor that is neither Soma nor brandy. The idea apparently is that Soma, the Benign God, is purchased in order to be slain; so, to escape the sin, the transaction is carried out in such a way that it is as if it had not taken place. On another occasion a piece of offering is buried where dry and moist meet so to to be neither on the ground nor in the water'.

We are reminded of the birth of Aphrodite, neither by day nor by night, but at dawn, neither on land nor in the water, but in the foam. We are thus now in a position to interpret the description of the Grail, 'not of wood, nor of any manner of metal, nor was it any wise of stone, nor of horn, nor of bone'. The guilt of the sacrifice must not adhere to any article or substance in common or ceremonial use. What this substance was—to borrow the same useful formula—is neither here nor there. There are many possibilities, but in Wolfram von Eschenbach's Parzifal it is described as 'Lapis Exillis', which could be read to be 'Lapis ex Caelis', or 'Lapis Lapsus ex Caelis', in other words a meteoric stone, the use of which would not communicate guilt to any earthly medium, but rather refer it back to the stars, or the gods. Alternatively it could have been Mother of Pearl, conceived as an emanation of the moon.

Continuing with Hocart as our immediate authority, 'Besides Soma figures a spirituous liquor, let us call it brandy. It plays, however, a very minor part; I only mention it here because of an important statement made by the Satapatha Brahma to the effect that 'Soma is drink, brandy is food.' What is meant by calling brandy food is not clear; the term food is evidently here used in a ritual sense.' Further, Hocart recalls Greek terminology. ' "Ambrosia" is the same word as "Amrita" and means "Immortality" . . . usually they called it nectar, and reserved the term ambrosia for food, but sometimes they spoke of eating nectar and drinking ambrosia.'

We here recall the reference in the prose Perceval to the maiden in the Grail procession who carried 'II tailleors d'argent'—two tailleors of silver. Miss Jessie Weston discusses this phenomenon on page 147-8 of *The Quest of the Holy Grail*. The word, as she points out, means a platter on which meat is carved. Wolfram von Eschenbach translates the term 'II tailleurs' as 'two silver knives,' and adds that they were very sharp. The ritual has no further use for such objects, and it is evident that the tailleurs held the food element of the sacrifice.

The coronation ritual is invariably followed by a feast, of which the Grail stories give full account. A further obligatory constituent of the ceremonial was the coronation procession, in which the newly crowned king conducts a tour of his kingdom. This is mentioned in ritual texts from early Egyptian times, and it is probable that until this royal circuit was completed the king was not regarded as being in full authority. Thus we can explain the situation which so puzzled Parzifal when he awoke on the morning following his failure to ask the vital question.

'He ran through many of the rooms, calling out for the people, but not a one did he hear or see . . . He ran out to where he had dismounted the evening before upon arrival. Here earth and grass were trampled down and the dew drops scattered . . . He found the gate wide open and through it the tracks of many horses leading out.'

One feature of the ceremonial has, we believe, not hitherto received notice. In the Perlesvaus version, dealing with the visit of Gawain to the Grail Castle, after he quite inexplicably fails to ask the cardinal question he is told, 'It was not of your own default that you would not speak the word whereof this castle would have been in joy'. Prior to this he has been defeated in a game of chess. (Branch VI Title XX).

Regarding games ritually played (in fact staged) on occasions when the cosmic drama required a royal victory, Hocart mentions (page 25 of *Kingship*) a game of dice that is played between the Dalai Lama of Thibet and the King of the Demons, where the dice are loaded in such a way that the former cannot fail to win. But further (*Ibid*, page 152) he reports an initiation ceremony held by a secret society (the Imandwa) of the Ruanda of Africa in which the leader, who impersonates L'Angomoe, the living god, wins his kingdom by playing a game of chess with a rival claimant to decide who will be king of the Imandwa.

V

From Kings and their divine relationships we must now turn to Gods and their earthly avatars. And we can confidently begin with the oldest records of Kingship.

Geb was the Egyptian Earth-God. At some time he may have been worshipped as the creator. He was notable for his power. He was the father of Osiris.

Osiris was the dead king. In his death he reaffirmed the continuity, or, to coin a term not particularly Egyptian, the stream of life through people and king, king and nature, nature and earth and creation. Because Osiris was natural growth, and was supported by his father the earth. Horus was the son of Osiris, and the legitimate king of Egypt.

This trilogy represents, in Mr Frankfort's words, 'an acknowledgement of the power in the earth and its relation to kingship'.

In the Memphite Theology, when Horus became king 'Osiris became earth in the Royal Castle . . . his son Horus appeared as king of Upper Egypt and as king of Lower Egypt in the arms of his father Osiris . . .' We note here the expression 'Royal Castle', which was Osiris' burial place at Memphis.

A text exists which is the script of a play performed at the accession of Senusert I. Mr Frankfort, describing this play in considerable detail, says, 'There is no doubt that it contains elements antedating the Middle Kingdom by many centuries.' The play was probably performed during the royal procession of the Pharaoh which took place between the date of the death of the king's predecessor and the new king's coronation (which, as we shall see, was linked with a great seasonal festival). In the course of this play, during Part VI, Horus embraces his dead father, and turning to Geb says, 'I hold in my embrace this my father who has become tired. May he become quite strong again.'

29

The 'dead' Osiris in his Djed pillar
being ritually supported by Horus
in the form of a hawk.
(Drawn by the author from a Middle Kingdom coffin.)
This sketch shows only the features
essential to the subject.
See 'Ritual Overtones in the Grail Legend'

It is explained that, in Egyptian euphemistic phraseology, 'to be ill' means 'to die', and 'to be tired' means 'to be dead'.

Osiris in death becomes divine, and 'supports' the new king and his land. Horus 'supports' his father, and this means that he gives him all the ritual aid needed for the peaceful entry of Osiris into immortality. But this scene also typifies the anxiety that the Egyptian felt over the uncertainty and mystery of death, an anxiety which overshadowed any fear there might be regarding the annual rising of the Nile. The Egyptians loved life, and were on the whole a happy people. This love and this happiness found expression in mortuary cults which eventually spread from royalty to the whole people. These concepts, if not the entire ritual—because Egyptian ritual was far too complex to bear transplantation in detail—reappear with extraordinary fidelity of detail among the society of the Grail Castle.

Always in the background there is the aged king. But when Parzival sets eyes on this king (Book V of Wolfram von Eschenbach) in a brief interlude, he sees 'the most beautiful old man he had ever beheld. I say it and do not exaggerate—he was greyer even than mist.'

In the same text, the sick lord of the castle, the son of the aforesaid aged king, 'had paid his debt to joy; his life was but a dying'. But in the 'Diu Crone', as recounted by Miss Weston, Gawain puts the required ritual question to this lord, and as soon as he does so 'the king springs up with a cry of joy: he was dead, but retained a semblance of life till the Quest was achieved. At daybreak he and his knights vanish'.

Thus in fact throughout the action both Grail kings were dead: with the rider that, in fact, they were both numbered among the immortals.

This appearance of Geb, Osiris, and the king-to-be (Gawain in earlier version, Parzifal in later) in manuscripts of the earlier second millenium A. D. is quite extraordinary, and would seem to require some intermediate stage or stages.

Nowhere but in ancient Egypt do we find the doctrine of the reigning king who becomes wholly divine on his accession. This aspect of kingship has little in common with Sir James Frazer's dying king, who is a ritual convenience in a primitive nature cult, and can be put to death by human means. Such a type of cult may certainly have lain in the mists of time behind the highly evolved Egyptian theology, and such cults outlived the fall of the age of the Gods. But the mortuary interest in Frazer's King of the Wood at Nemi, for instance, is non-existent.

It is significant that the relationship Osiris-Horus is re-enacted in that of Enlil to Ninurta and Marduk to Nabu in Mesopotamian beliefs.

Egyptian religious ideas exerted considerable influence on Canaanite thought in later days, and Canaanite thought was apparently a formative factor in Persian religious evolution. We find the three kings of our ritual exemplified in the legendary, or quasi-historical Persian personages of Kai Kaus, his son Siyavosh who was murdered by Afrasiyab, the Seth of this story, and his grandson Kai Khusrau, who avenged Siyavosh and ascended the throne. But the grand design has now become biographic, adapted to the uses of the story-teller, and there is only a confused reflection of a religious ritual.

The Fisher King, or rather the peculiar title he bears, has been one of the most troublesome thorns in the flesh of Grail students. Setting aside the 'fertility cult fish meal' theory, we find the first relevant clue in the writings of Sir J. C. Coyajee, who associated the title with the search for the Royal Glory, referred to in Section 3 above. Here the Royal Glory is described as growing at the bottom of the sea Vouru-Kasha, and the narration features Afrasiyab, the

An Akkadian Seal
showing a God being liberated from a mountain.
(see "Ritual Overtones in the Grail Legend")

Japanese Incense Burner in the Shape of a Nat House
These latter are still common in the wilder parts of South-east Asia. Nats are averse to visitors who wash, and in fact to innovation generally, and do not aspire to a wider social life. Their standard of living, by progressive standards, is deplorably low.
(see "Dark Frontier")

Japanese scroll drawing dated 1836 showing the dragon as a beneficent spirit swimming in his native waters. Not to be confused with the Monster of Chaos, drought, and flood, which usually possessed numerous heads, signifying destructive power and confusion. (see "Sources of the Great Flood")

pretender to the throne of Iran, stripping himself naked and diving for it.

This concept of the Royal Glory is in itself, as we pointed out, as vague and elusive as the object itself. However, Sir J. C. Coyajee goes on to associate the act of diving for the Royal Glory with the Indian myth of the Churning of the Ocean, and here we believe that he lit on the true interpretation, though in fact he did not follow it to its logical conclusion.

The tale of the Churning of the Ocean in Indian mythology is a creation story. The myth of the creation of the world from soil delved out of the ocean bed is one of the commonest renderings of this theme, though in Indian theology it has been cast in a somewhat esoteric form. The Indian gods are said to have grasped the Cosmic Mountain (i.e. the axis of the world) and stirred the primordial ocean with it. The principal agent was Vishnu, who, in the form of a turtle, supported the axis, and the latter was twirled by a rope formed of the ocean-circling serpent of ancient mythologies. Among the products of this operation was Amrita. In another story, Vishnu completed the creation of the cosmos by means of three ritual strides, and this action forms a stage in the early Egyptian coronation ceremony.

The twirling process employed is repeated in the method already referred to of mixing the divine or royal Soma, and the sacrifice of preparing and mixing Soma appears to have itself constituted a re-creation ceremony. Incidentally it is of interest that there is a Kalmuk myth which relates that the gods used Sumer as a stick to stir the ocean, thus creating the sun, moon, and stars. (Mircea Eliade—*Shamanism*, page 267).

We can now see how the Grail cup, the Soma vessel, came to be associated with the Fisher King. The latter in his earliest known manifestation was Geb, the Egyptian

God of Earth, and one-time God of Creation. He fished in the primordial ocean for the world, and having taken Nut the sky goddess for wife produced the earthly gods of nature and kingship.

The habitat of the Fisher King, as creation and ancestor god, was the underworld. The Grail Castle has many parallels in folk lore, where it features as a castle below the sea, on a mountain of ice, etc. The approach to the Grail Castle is described in similar terms to the perilous road along which the primitive Shaman guided the souls of the dead to their place in the underworld.

For instance, in Siberia the spirit of the dead had to cross 'a bridge the breadth of a hair.' In Malaya, 'a tree-trunk stripped of its bark, over a cauldron of boiling water.' In North America, 'A bridge that constantly shakes and moves.' In Persia and Arab tradition it was the Kinvat Bridge, and in the prose Edda 'the Bridge Gjallar.'

In the Perlesvaus version of the Grail story, Gawain, approaching the castle, has to negotiate 'three bridges, right great and right horrible to pass'. 'Three great waters run below.' The first bridge is 'a bowshot in length, and in breadth not more than a foot.' The second bridge is 'of ice, feeble and thin, and of a great height above the water'.

In the Bleheris/Blihis version, Gawain's approach to the Grail Castle is through the Waste Land to a seashore, where he comes to a causeway, arched over by trees, leading far out into the sea and washed over by waves. At the end glimmers a light. He tries to stop his horse, but is carried over the causeway to the castle against his will.

In another episode of the legend, Lancelot has to cross a similar bridge—in fact the edge of a sword.

VI

We now have to consider a further quest, the particulars of

34

which will help to dispose of a number of outstanding puzzles in the Grail legend. But this quest is not to be considered an alternative solution, or a mere confusion in the 'folk memory' of one issue with another. It is an integral concomitant of the quest we have hitherto been considering.

Miss Jessie Weston compared the lamenting women of the Grail procession with the women who were said to lament the death of Adonis, or Tammuz, and founded on this detail among others her theory of a Syrian or Mesopotamian type fertility cult.

Lewis Richard Farnell, in *Greek Hero Cults and Ideas of Immortality*, differentiates pertinently between at least two types of ritual lament. There was, for example, the name which was nothing more than the mere 'projection' of a dirge, such as Ialemos, a wail personalised, or perhaps Hulas (a Bithnynian vegetation spirit) which produces an appropriately gloomy sound. Frazer writes in *The Golden Bough* of the Lityerses Song, and of the wail of the Devon farmer as he cut the last sheaves—'Wee yen, way yen'.

To these shadow creations, as Mr. Farnell says, no real myth or no state-ritual attaches.

When Osiris was murdered and his body spirited away in highly ritual fashion in a specially constructed chest, Isis and Nepthys went in search of him, calling continually 'come to the house'.

We can call this a ritual search, and in its early Egyptian form it is for the King-God of vegetation.

In *The Nine Songs*, a study of Shamanism in Ancient China, Mr Waley gives examples of a literary development of this concept. In these poems, the Shaman is summoning and speaking with a god or powerful spirit. The interview is brief. Alas, the god is capricious, and does not scruple to depart after his brief flirtation, leaving his devotee desolate and empty.

Song III. The Princess of the Shiang
I will deck myself in all my handsome finery
And set out to find her, riding in my cassie-boat . . .
I look towards the Princess, but she does not come;
Blowing her pan-pipes there, of whom is she thinking? . . .
In the morning I gallop my horses through the lowlands
    by the River;
In the evening I stay my course at that northern shore.

Song IV. The Lady of the Shiang
Someone says that my lovely one has sent for me;
I will mount my chariot and let him bring me to her.

Song V. The Big Lord of Lives
The gates of Heaven are open wide;
Off I ride, borne on a dark cloud! . . .
Why think that his task is among *us*?
High he flies, peacefully winging . . .

Song IX. The Mountain Spirit
It seems there is someone over there, in that fold of the hill,
Clad in creepers, with a belt of mistletoe.

He is gazing at me, his lips parted in a smile;
'Have you taken a fancy to me? Do I please you with
    my lovely ways?' . . .
Driving red leopards, followed by stripy civets,
Chariot of magnolia, banners of cassia . . .
I go, gathering sweet herbs to give to the one I love . . .
The way was perilous and hard; that is why I am late
    for the tryst . . .
Waiting for the Divine One I linger, and forget to go back.

The search for an absent god played an exceptional
part in the religious concepts and practices of the Hittites.
These are subjected to detailed analysis in Theodor H.
Gaster's *Thespis, Ritual, Myth and Drama in the Ancient*

Near East (Harper Torchbooks).

The myth of Telipinu tells the story of the withdrawal of the god of fertility, and the search instituted for him. After a preliminary discussion at a divine banquet, the gods 'great and small' conduct an extensive search for the missing god. When this proves unsuccessful, an eagle is dispatched, but his mission is equally fruitless. A bee is then sent out, and this insect finds Telipinu, asleep in a forest. The god, however, is furious at being awakened, and will not return. Magical remedies are employed to sooth his wrath, and he is welcomed back to the world of gods and men.

'The Telipinu text', says Mr Gaster, 'represents but one form of a procedure current among the Hittites in times of disaster. The latter was believed to be due to the withdrawal of an offended deity, and the purpose of the procedure was to secure his return. In sister versions virtually the same myth and ritual are associated with a number of other gods and with personal as well as national calamities.'

Another myth concerns the ravages of a malevolent being called Hahhimas. This demon is identified with frost. A goddess asks the supreme god to intervene, and the latter orders the sun to be summoned. The sun, however, cannot be found. A number of gods go in search of the sun, but one by one they fall victim to Hahhimas. At this point the demon tells the supreme god that he is losing his grip on the royal chalice. The story is broken off at this point, when a further mission is about to set forth.

In other Middle Eastern texts, as for instance in the Canaanite Baal legends, the searcher is the sun god or goddess.

In Mesopotamia the New Year festival was the cardinal religious event of the year. Frankfort says, 'The recital of the gods' victory over chaos at the beginning of time cast a spell of accomplishment over the hazardous and all-important renewal of natural life in the present'. Quoting A. J. Wensinck in *The Semitic New Year and the Origin of Eschatology*, he continues, 'the association is preserved in the link which Jewish tradition lays between the creation of the world and the New Year's festivities in Tishri and Nisan, both of them the beginning of a new harvest'.

Mourning to the accompaniment of ritual wailings took place at the intermediate season, in the stifling heat of May and June. The mourning goddess gave herself up to laments in which the people joined:

The wailing for him who is far away—for he may not come.

At the New Year, when the grip of death over the land is broken, the return of the god is celebrated with psalms of joy

> He is announced at the gate of the land;
>   he returns to his place!
> He approaches the gate of the land;
>   he returns to his place!

In the Babylonian celebration, on the fifth day of the feast, is held a Day of Atonement for the king. The search for Marduk then begins, and altogether disrupts the city. On the sixth day Nabu, the son and avenger of Marduk, in the person of the king, arrives in the city, and on the seventh day he liberates Marduk by force from the 'mountain' of the Netherworld. (Frankfort's reconstruction in *Kingship and the Gods,* page 318).

Marduk is not the only Mesopotamian fertility god to be confined in, and rescued from, a 'mountain'. In a Sumerian text, Lillu, 'the weak one' calls to his 'sister', a goddess, from a similar place of confinement 'The place where I rest is the dust of the mountain'.

In Babylon, the 'mountain' was probably the Ziggurat, the temple tower, symbol of the earth, or the Netherworld, from which in due course the suffering God would be ritually liberated.

It is significant that one of the texts mentions a person or god who has 'ridden to the mountain'.

In Assyria, the king represented the divine hero Ninurta (the Assyrian equivalent of Nabu) and entered the royal city in a chariot.

The connection (of which only a few examples are given here out of the many available) between the act of creation of the world and the New Year celebrations, and the assumption by the king of the role of the son of God, emphasises a vital aspect of Near Eastern religions which is frequently overlooked.

These religions, both in ancient Egypt and Mesopotamia, were in essence cosmic, in that the High God and the fertility god were merged in the supreme god, and in the king where he represented or incarnated this god. Thus the High God embodied both the powers of the earth—expressed in the fertility of nature—and those of the sun, at least in the later evolution of those religions.

The two functions are, in fact, mutually exclusive, since the sun has never been regarded as an instrument of fertility. Elliot Smith derived the cult of sun worship from the invention of the Solar (or Sothic) calendar. The sun came to be regarded as the supreme maintainer of truth (as revealed by the light) as against the darkness of ignorance; of order as against chaos; and, by derivation, of good as against evil. In what we prefer to call the Age of War, the sun came to represent the victory of these qualities over the powers of chaos, among which were counted the enemies of the state.

One certainly could not now follow Elliot Smith's ideas to their logical conclusion, and Hocart also placed too much emphasis on the Solar cults. After all, though the victory of order over chaos is unquestionably the *fons et origo* of all public religion, it was expressed quite differently in early Mesopotamia, where the victorious god, who defeats the 'Monster' (not the Dragon) of Chaos, is Lord of the atmosphere, of thunder and rain, in keeping with an environment in which the sun might at any time adopt the unwelcome role of 'the man who stayed for dinner'.

Nevertheless, the storm god, Enlil, whose cult under various names, spread over the Middle East as far as Anatolia and Persia, became himself the symbol of order and light, and assumed solar functions.

This question is well discussed in Ivan Engnell's work *Studies in Divine Kingship in the Ancient Near East* (Blackwood). This author also examines, in their separate contexts, the seasonal festivals as they are celebrated under the varying climatic conditions of the vast Middle Eastern area.

Some of these were held in the spring, and some in the autumn, at the close of the hot weather. Among the Hittites, celebrations appear to have been held at both solstices. A feature of all these festivals, of immediate concern to the subject of this essay, was the enthronement of the king.

The Egyptian practice, however, extended to the act of coronation. At whatever time of year a new king was invested with sovereignty, his coronation was deferred until the New Year. (Frankfort—*Kingship and the Gods*).

VII

As far as the provenance of the oriental sources of the Grail legend are concerned, Professor Loomis' observations are of value. That is to say, they could well have been conveyed to Europe with the Arab invasion.

More thought should perhaps be given to the vast area covered by Persia in its heyday, and the extent of Persian influence upon the Middle East and Eastern Europe. Persia was the peer of Rome, and, like Rome, a conveyor of cultures, though as an originator of arts and literature she was more comparable with China and India, perhaps even Greece. The Persia of the Sassanids fell to the Arab conquest, which carried much of the detritus of that great empire across North Africa into Spain.

The whole concept of the 'Waste Land' is foreign to Northern European climate and conditions. The devastating droughts or floods implied are familiar hazards in Southern Asia, and have always been so: river floods have only constituted a risk in Europe under modern conditions of land drainage and preservation, and, of course, deforestation.

It is fascinating to turn, for a last moment, to the Persian elements in the stories we are considering. Though there is, in fact, no trace of Mithraic ritual, as far as we know anything about it, there is much material still to be considered in the Shah Nameh.

For instance, there was a great warrior who was instrumental in finding Kai Khusrau and bringing him back from his childhood exile to assume the crown of Iran. His name was Giw, in the Pahlavi is Gevan, and in Zend Gaevani. This hero could equate with Gawain. Parzifal, or Perceval, could be simply 'the Persian'.

Merlin, who prophesied that he would end his life on earth by being entombed by enchantment, is evidently a misplacement in the story of the Suffering God entombed in a mountain. His name is claimed in Welsh as Myrddin, but this also, as Mir Din, is a respectable and still quite common Persian name, and means 'Religious leader'.

SOURCES OF THE GREAT FLOOD

AND ITS DIFFUSION

Just as there is no historical source, even though it may have
been used for centuries, that has yielded everything it contains, so there is no fundamental fact whose truth or falsity
has been tested by all the means available to us.

J. J. Bachofen

I

The text which contains the Egyptian story of the Flood dates from the time of the New Kingdom: however, internal evidence would relegate it to a far earlier period, since mass human sacrifice on the harvest fields, on the Aztec model, is not recorded in the historical age of Egypt.

The great god RA is beginning to manifest signs of old age, and in consequence his people are conspiring against him. On the advice of the council of Gods, he sends his eye, in the person of the Mother Goddess Hathor, to destroy the rebels.

Not being familiar with the English military doctrine of Minimum Force, Hathor launches out into an interminable slaughter of the human race. This must clearly be stopped, since the human race is necessary for the maintenance of the gods. RA therefore orders the preparation of a large quantity of beer, coloured with red ochre to simulate blood. This is poured over the fields, and when Hathor rises to continue her work of killing, she drinks the brew, thinking it to be blood, and becomes intoxicated. Thereafter the killing stops, and in the sequel she is served with intoxicants on all the occasions of her feast days, becoming *inter alia* the earliest recorded Goddess of Wine.

The part played by RA in this story recalls the customs associated with the character of the Dying God, so amply treated by Sir James Frazer. He deals at length with the occurrence of substitution, to which we shall refer later. However, it is probable that RA himself is a later interpolation in a very old story, since the Goddess of Nature can claim primacy in primitive fertility beliefs. The text itself may, perhaps, be interpreted as a story of priestly provenance devised to explain the offering of intoxicants to a nature goddess. More probably, and of more immediate concern to the subject of this study—it is of interest largely as illustrating the idea of substitution, and there are many episodes in the mythology of other lands and ages that provide parallels.

In the first essay in this volume, we referred to an episode in the history of ANAT, the Canaanite Nature Goddess. Here her fury extends to inanimate objects, and it is worth considering that these may, in fact, have been substitute victims. The tales related of Isaac and Iphigenie and their abortive sacrifice provide classic examples of substitution; and to carry the subject into other realms of religion and superstitious observance, one can instance the dolls that were provided for young children in ancient Japan to act as targets for the evil eye, the custom of the couvade or the simulacrum of the deceased that featured in Roman funerary ritual.

Many rituals current in classical times embodied a pretence of human sacrifice. A very recent treatment of this class of rite can be found in *Myths and Symbols: Studies in Honour of Mircea Eliade*, published by the University of Chicago Press, in an essay by Angelo Brelich entitled *Symbol of a Symbol*. This essay suggests that even the Foundation Myth which relates to a ritual of symbolic human sacrifice, located as it is in a mythological period, may have reference to a sacrifice which was itself symbolic, such as the pretended killing of novices at initiation, or the killing of a sacred animal.

The higher religions of later historical times have, indeed, reawakened the anger of the Gods, and Noah's flood may even now be invoked as a warning from the pulpit to a rebellious or degenerate generation. The priest-ridden and declining culture of the Aztecs would appear to have re-armed an impotent tradition or an innocent symbol. Because not the least charge that can be brought against latter-day man is that he is too fanatical, too serious, too committed.

II

Yima, in early Persian religion, was the first man and the first King of the Dead. In his introduction to Fargard II of the *Zend Avesta,* James Darmesteter, the translator in the edition prepared under the direction of Max Muller, wrote:

> The world, lasting a long year of twelve milleniums, was to end by a dire winter, like the Eddic Fimbul winter, to be followed by an everlasting spring, when men, sent back to earth from the heavens, should enjoy, in an eternal earthly life, the same happiness that they had enjoyed after their death in the realm of Yima. But as in the definitive form which was taken by Mazdean cosmology the world was made to end by fire, its destruction by winter was no longer the last incident of its life, and therefore the Var of Yima, instead of remaining, as it was originally, the paradise that gives back to earth its inhabitants, came to be nothing more than a sort of Noah's Ark.

From the Introduction to Volume I of the *Zend Avesta,* in the same edition, the following passage (Para. 38) expands on this concept:

> But, by and by, as it was forgotten that Yima was the first man and the first of the dead, it was also forgotten that his people were nothing else than the dead going

to their common ancestor above and to the king of heaven: the people in the Vara were no longer recognised as the human race, but became a race of a supernatural character, different from those who continued going, day by day, from earth to heaven to join Ahura Mazda.

Fargard II contains the instructions given to Yima by Ahura Mazda, and his compliance therewith:

22 (46). And Ahura Mazda spake unto Yima, saying:
'O fair Yima, son of Vivanghat! Upon the material world the fatal winters are going to fall, that shall bring the fierce, foul frost; upon the material world the fatal winters are going to fall, that shall make snowflakes fall thick, even an aredvi deep on the highest tops of mountains.'

23 (52). 'And all the three sorts of beasts shall perish, those that live in the wilderness, and those that live on the tops of the mountains, and those that live in the bosom of the dale, under the shelter of stables.'

24 (57). 'Before that winter, those fields would bear plenty of grass for cattle; now with floods that stream, with snows that melt, it will seem a happy land in the world, the land wherein footprints even of sheep may still be seen.'

25 (61). 'Therefore make thee a Vara, long as a riding-ground on every side of the square, and thither bring the seeds of sheep and oxen, of men, of dogs, of birds, and of red blazing fires.'
'Therefore make thee a Vara, long as a riding-ground on every side of the square, to be an abode for men; a Vara, long as a riding-ground on every side of the square, to be a fold for flocks.'

26 (65). 'There thou shalt make waters flow in a bed a hathra long; there thou shalt settle birds, by the ever-green banks that bear never-failing food.'

27 (70). 'Thither thou shalt bring the seeds of men and women, of the greatest, best, and finest kinds on this earth; thither thou shalt bring the seeds of every kind of cattle, of the greatest, best, and finest kinds on this earth.'

28 (74). 'Thither thou shalt bring the seeds of every kind of tree, of the greatest, best, and finest kinds on this earth; thither thou shalt bring the seeds of every kind of fruit, the fullest of food and sweetest of odour. All those seeds shalt thou bring, two of every kind, to be kept inexhaustible there, so long as those men shall stay in the Vara.'

30 (87). 'In the largest part of the place thou shalt make nine streets, six in the middle part, three in the smallest. To the streets of the largest part thou shalt bring a thousand seeds of men and women; to the streets of the middle part, six hundred; to the streets of the smallest part, three hundred. That Vara thou shalt seal up with the golden ring, and thou shalt make a door, and a window self-shining within.'

In his study of the Flood story and its world-wide diffusion, Sir James Frazer (*Folk Lore in the Old Testament*) remarks on the fact that the Book of Genesis contains two distinct Destruction stories, the Flood itself, of which Noah was the survivor, and the episode of the destruction of Sodom and Gomorrah, in which Lot and his family were destined to be spared. The story of Noah evidently derives from the Mesopotamian version as recounted in the Gilgamesh epic. Noah himself is not pictured as an Immortal, as is his prototype Utnapishtim, and the latter is seen to be equated with Yima, and the Vedic Yama. The tale of Lot does not possess the charm of the Flood story, with its ark and its dove, although it is a more useful instrument in the hands of headmasters. There would be a strong temptation to disassociate it altogether from the subject of this essay were it not for the preference for fire displayed in the Persian writings quoted above, and for the variant of the destruction myth that is contained in the Book of Revelations.

We should by now be well accustomed to the itinerant habits of ideas, and the Book of Revelations has wandered far from the severe and monumental judgement hall of Osiris. In fact, it contains little Judgement and much purgation and is in part the description of a ritual of Initiation. 'What are these that are arrayed in white robes, and whence came they?' 'These are they that came out of great tribulation, and have washed their robes in the blood of the Lamb.' We can see here something of the effect of the transformation, in the course of development of Persian moral and legalistic thought, of the simple dead, the original inheritors of the Afterworld, into the Elect. We can also recognise, in the description of the New Jerusalem, the city built by Yima in the Vara; not a New City, but an eternal city, prefabricated to ride out the storm.

That this refuge of the Elect represented also an early sectarian view of heaven, only a heaven which was the final and eternal goal of the human soul, is patent. Such also was the Castle of the Grail, of which we have treated. In some aspects of the story of this Castle, the dire winter to which we referred above has survived intact, to strike a note of astonishing incongruity. When Parsifal quits the Castle after his first visit, he finds himself floundering in deep snow, which is not at all the picture of the Waste Land elsewhere portrayed, and for the resuscitation of which the Suffering God is to be sought and rescued.

Forty years ago we could have found numbers of stout men of war from the Ritualistic camp of mythological dialectic, ready and eager to enlarge this glimpse of Initiation into a general Initiation theory, designed to cover the destruction myths as a whole. But it is more likely that the identifiable sources of St John's vision were twofold. First, there was an Initiation ceremony, a Mystery possibly of Mithraic type; and secondly there was a theory of human perpetuance, stemming from, or allied to, Egyptian concepts, and not found in early Mesopotamian belief.

A ritual death followed by a rebirth forms the basis of all initiation ceremonies, and is an almost universal feature of tribal life. The concept of a sacred city, however, could only arise in an urbanised environment. The Egyptian, who never developed much of a domestic architecture, thought of the ideal after-life in terms of a pastoral and agricultural elysium: though in fact, without any notion that he was postulating a contradiction, he also conceived of death as an absorption into the eternal cycle of natural and cosmic forces, the union with the life of the great gods so carefully prepared for his kings. This formed the motive behind all·his funerary ritual, but the concept itself merely reflected his total obsession with what in English clerical circles used to be entertained in terms of the 'wider hope'.

Any theory based on the supposition that there could have been a ritual of destruction corresponding to known rituals of re-creation contains a fundamental fallacy. Fire and water, in early religious and magical belief, were the instruments respectively of purgation and lustration. Purgation was a measure employed at critical or seasonal junctures to expel evil and prepare for new activity or growth. Evil had to be driven out of the community, as in the custom of the scapegoat. Water was a divine agent which had, as we shall see later, to be kept out of the hands of evil agents. The idea of either as an instrument of divine retribution belongs in every case to a later degeneration of religious concepts. Rites of initiation provided for the ritual death of the novice, followed by his immediate resurrection. Rites of purgation of holy places involved the destruction of the old sacrifice, as instanced in European Spring ceremonies of removing the previous year's May Tree, or even the replacement of the temple furniture. The temple itself could not be destroyed, and where a site had for any reason become ritually contaminated or taboo, a new temple was built elsewhere. Some cultures practised a periodical migration of this kind, as for instance in Japan, where the grove and temples of Ise are removed to a new site every twenty years. Above all, the homeland, its cities and fields, its gods, temples, and ancestors, are held universally to be sacred.

III

The moon and water, in ancient belief, are if not bisexual, of equivocal sex. Water is masculine because its operations are analogous to those of male sperm. It is feminine because it can be seen to be controlled by the moon, which is subject to monthly fluctuations. The moon likewise is held to be masculine in some cultures, and feminine in others. It is masculine because it controls the movement of water, regarded in its masculine aspect. It is feminine because it follows a monthly pattern of change. The denizens of water partake of the equivocal sex of water itself, shells, for instance, have been regarded as feminine by virtue of their resemblance to the vulva, or masculine in consideration of the virile and fecund note of the conch trumpet, still to be heard sounded in Indian temples at the approach of a storm.

Thus, for instance, the moon in Japan is a God, and the sun is a Goddess, while in adjacent China the sexes are reversed. It was apparently more usual for the moon to be regarded as feminine in early Neolithic cultures, and before the days of heavy agriculture, when the garden was regarded as the special province of women. Much of the charm of early classic—Greek and Cretan—tradition is that it penetrates so deeply into early cultural horizons, one of which provides us with the goddesses of gardens and trees. It may be that the balance of opinion was for a feminine moon, suggested by the analogy between a waxing moon and pregnancy.

Hathor, in the story recounted in the first part of this study, when the concoction of beer and colouring matter is poured out before her, expresses pleasure at the sight of her reflected face and is seen to float serenely on the water's surface. Elliot Smith, treating of this episode in *The Evolution of the Dragon*, takes it to be the prototype of all flood stories, the surrogate sacrifice followed by the appearance of the Mother God riding the waters to restore fertility to the thirsty Nile Valley. There is evidence, which we will examine now, to support this proposition, but as we hope to show, it cannot be stretched to cover the whole of the flood story in its classic form, still less its variants and the versions that may have been diffused across the world.

In Fargard XXI of the *Zend-Avesta,* in the edition already quoted, which is devoted to Waters and Light, in paragraph 9, occurs the following invocation:

Up! Rise up, thou moon, that dost keep in thee the seed
of the bull . . . and produce light for the world . . .

And an editorial comment on this passage says—'When the bull died, what was bright and strong in his seed was brought to the sphere of the moon, and when it was cleansed there in the light of the astre, two creatures were shaped with it, a male and a female, from which came two hundred and seventy-two kinds of animals'.

And in Paragraph 4 of the *Mah Yast* occurs the sentence, 'And when the light of the moon waxes warmer, golden-hued plants grow on from the earth during the spring'.

The *Zend-Avesta* has, of course, survived in very fragmentary form, and it is not possible to extract from available texts the complete doctrine to which the above quotations refer. The moon itself is referred to in the female gender. The bull was symbolic of the virile powers of nature, a symbol which occurred throughout the Middle East from Greece and Crete, through Anatolia, as far East as Tibet and India. It was generally regarded not so much as a God, as a vehicle of divine potency. It could die, and suffer sacrifice.

Though in the above references the moon is pictured as a repository or ark which held the seeds of plants and animals, there is no suggestion that it was a boat, after the Egyptian concept of the sun on its daily journey, nor yet a chariot drawn by horses, stags, or oxen. Rather is the replenishment of the world seen as the product of a parturition at full moon. The ancient theological mind might, however, find less difficulty in equating the Persian with the Egyptian concept than later commentators schooled in a severer criticism.

A reconciliation in some sort between the Persian and the Egyptian versions can be found in the details of the Dionysia as described by Thucydides. Dionysus is reported to have arrived in Greece 'from the East', and his cult may have been introduced by way of Ionia, though his legend is also associated with Minoan Crete. The bull was his sacred animal, and he was revered in the form of a bull. At the Athenian festival his image was carried in a wheeled ship, one variant of a very wide-spread celebration. A ship of the Gods was conducted throughout the Nile lands in ancient

Egypt, and was thought to bring with it good fortune and fertility wherever it went. A wheeled ship is a familiar feature of Mediterranean carnivals, and the ship, with or without wheels, was widely held to be sacred in ancient times. Rock carvings of the bronze age period in Sweden show ships in association with the sacred axe, and also with a tree planted in mid vessel, which could be the Tree of Life.

The festival, naturally enough, was largely concerned with wine drinking, though Dionysus embodied the wider aspects of Nature. A commentary on it, and certain cognate aspects of it, is provided by John Pollard in *Seers, Shrines and Sirens*. He says, 'The third day of the Anthesteria' (the February celebrations) 'is very mysterious and has provoked much controversy. It was called the Chytroi or 'Porridge Pot', and began on the evening of the Choes. But its mood, to judge from the authorities, was far from convivial. Indeed we are assured that it was a day of gloom and associated with the dead, who had perished in Deucalion's (the Greek Noah's) flood'. Mr Pollard discusses the injunction that was seemingly addressed to the dead at the end of the day's festival—'Out of doors carians (or Keres) the Anthesteria is over'—and suggests that the last day of the celebrations may fortuitously have coincided with a separate festival of the dead: alternatively that vestiges of an underworld tradition clung to the person of Dionysus.

It is possible that the 'Porridge Pots' are none other than the 'Mother Pots' associated with the Egyptian mother goddess. Of the 'victims of the flood' we have already spoken. We do not hear of an act of mourning in connection with the Egyptian version of the story, but this latter is fragmentary. Not being renewed in custom, being in any case probably a fiction, it may have been forgotten.

This essay makes use as far as possible of literary sources, since these are the earliest we have, and are fairly distinct, in contrast with those collected orally in our own time, which are inclined to confuse their subject matter, betraying in this the effect of a long process of diffusion in space and time. Thus, for instance, flood stories, gathered among illiterate communities, are frequently confused with myths of creation. It is, nevertheless, perhaps relevant to compare the Persian version of the part played by the moon with that of a sea-faring people. In Maori legend, for instance, the 'first woman', Hina, was identified with the moon, and became Hina-the-watchwoman, guardian of travellers. She was herself a great traveller, and in Tahiti was called 'Hina-the-canoe-pilot'. She was also goddess of the underworld, and the mother of a large variety of creatures. Her destructive aspect was represented by the Hawaiian volcano goddess Pele, also a great traveller. It may be legitimate to associate the Polynesian moon/mother goddess with the spirit canoe of allied myths which was paddled by a crew of ancestors.

IV

Information about the customs and beliefs of peoples that follow archaic ways of life has been collected within very recent centuries, except where random references can be culled from the writings of classic—e.g. Greek and Roman writers. Information about the earliest known urban societies is now available as far back as the third millenium. Thus, except where there are even earlier pictographic records, and some tentative interpretation of these has been possible, it has not been easy to determine the primacy of archaic customs and traditions.

Sometimes when material is gathered near the fountain-head, it can be recognised as a true source. Sometimes also a concept can be attributed to known developments in human techniques and conditions of life, as when we have a God of Maize or Corn.

Certain Mesopotamian and allied myths, for instance, can be directly related to conditions prevailing in those emergent civilisations. The Ras Shamra tablets give an account of the campaign waged by Baal to subdue the destructive activities of the sea:

Have I not smitten sea, beloved of El?
Have I not annihilated Ocean Current, the great God?

Then soars and swoops the mace in the hand of Baal,
Even as an eagle in his fingers.
It smites the shoulders of Prince Sea,
Even the breast of Ocean Current the Ruler.

The quotations are extracted from the excellent essay by Mr John Gray in *Near Eastern Mythology*.

Closer to our subject, however, is one of the earliest datable myths in existence. Kur features as the Monster of Chaos in Sumerian writings, and some of the tales which refer to him have only very recently been pieced together by Samuel Noah Kramer, from whose handbook *Sumerian Mythology* I quote. Kur is perhaps the prototype of all those monsters whose slaying was the achievement of national and racial heroes, such as Baal, Perseus, 'St George', or their bird equivalents, the Indian Garuda, the Burmese Galon, etc. In later mythologies this was the monster which held back the life-giving rain, and its slayer was the God of Upper Air, or the Storm. In the variant of the Kur stories which we quote, the hero was Ninurta, the warrior god, son of Enlil, the God of Air. Ninurta succeeds in killing the monster, as a result of which 'The primeval waters which Kur had held in check rise to the surface, and as a result of their violence no fresh water can reach the fields and gardens. The gods of the land who 'carried the pick-axe and the basket', that is, who had charge of irrigating the land and preparing it for cultivation, are desperate'.

> Famine was severe, nothing was produced,
> The small rivers were not cleansed,
> the dirt was not carried off.

To continue Mr Kramer's account—'Ninurta sets up a heap of stones over the dead Kur and heaps it up like a great wall in front of the land. These stones hold back the "mighty waters".' Ninurta then gathers the waters which had already flooded the land, and leads them into the Tigris.

The interest of this myth lies in its close account of the processes of raising levees against the tides, and of engineering or restoring fresh-water irrigation channels. It illustrates an initial exposition or dramatisation of an actual agricultural problem on the part of the earliest economy known to have practised irrigation: it is explicit and straightforward and does not introduce irrelevant characters.

Probably the most definitive collection of Flood stories is still that published by Sir James Frazer in *Folk Lore in the Old Testament*. Gathered from all over the world, these are remarkable for their length, their strange and widely varied circumstances, and their mass of 'pretty' and irrelevant detail. There are, to be sure, considerable areas of the world where no flood of any consequence has been reported, such as Europe and Japan. Generally, however, the stories are widely diffused, and we will now refer to a few reported from Indonesia, Australia, Oceania, and America, selecting those which ascribe the calamity to causes which could not possibly occur spontaneously to any person, at any cultural level, not in the grip of dementia or delirium tremens.

In Cochin China, a primitive tribe called the Bahnars believed that a flood, whose waters reached the sky, came out of a hole in a crab's skull.

The Sea Dyaks of Borneo told how some Dyak women

tried to cut bamboo shoots from what they took to be a fallen bamboo, but which turned out to be a giant boa-constrictor. The men of the tribe killed the serpent, it was cut up and taken home to cook, when a torrential rain began to fall, and caused a flood which killed everyone in the world except the few inevitable survivors, in this case a woman, a dog, and a rat.

The aborigines of Lake Eyers in Victoria, Australia, believed that all the water in the world was swallowed by a huge frog, and the other animals could only force it to disgorge by making it laugh. A pelican in a canoe rescued a few survivors.

In New Guinea there were two floods, the second of which resulted from the eating of a huge fish.

The Jibaros of Ecuador tell how some crocodile hunters killed a young crocodile, thus angering the mother, who caused a flood by lashing her tail.

In Algonquin legend the flood occurred as a consequence of the killing of a white lynx, or 'water lynx', a mythical animal, and the Ojibways of Southern Ontario told a similar story about a 'water lion'.

The Cree Indians relate the tale of a sea monster who conceived a hatred for a very wise enchanter, and sought to destroy him by lashing the sea with his tail till the whole earth was flooded.

In Tinnen Indian legend, an inexplicable flood was brought to an end by a bittern, which swallowed all the water. A plover scratched the bittern's stomach, upon which the bittern disgorged the water into the rivers and lakes.

An interesting Tlingit story goes that Raven had put a woman under the world to attend to the rising and falling of the tides. Wishing to find out what goes on under the sea, he caused the woman to raise the water, and the world was flooded but for the mountain-tops.

V

At a Mandan ceremony witnessed by Catlin, held to comm-
emorate the flood, 'the first or only man who escaped the
flood was personated by a mummer dressed in a robe of
white wolf-skins'. This mummer toured the village, relating
the story of the flood of which he was the sole survivor,
and collected an edged tool of some kind from every household. In the evening the collection was deposited in the
medicine lodge which was opened once a year for this
purpose, and on the last day of the rites was thrown into a
deep pool as a sacrifice to the Spirit of the Water. It was
explained that 'If this is not done there will be another
flood, and no one will be saved, as it was with such tools
that the big canoe was made'. The ceremony was accompanied by a bull dance, the object of which was to ensure
a plentiful supply of buffalo during the coming year, and an
ordeal, or purgation of initiation type undergone by the
young men of the village. Were all these rites not performed,
there would be another flood. The 'big canoe' referred to
was the vessel in which the survivor of the flood landed on
a mountain top.

The bull dance, as Frazer remarks, may only have been
fortuitously associated with the flood ceremony. The flood
referred to in this account reads, of course, like a typical
'myth to explain a ritual'.

The whole proceeding possesses an orderliness and logic
not found elsewhere, and gives a strong impression of primacy. But there is a lapse of some 3,000 to 5,000 years
between the recording of this story and the writing of our
Middle Eastern sources.

VI

The Mesopotamian flood story is available in Sumerian

texts in extremely fragmentary form. The hero was Zius-
udra, a pious king who obtained immortality. His counterpart in the more complete version in the Gilgamesh epic,
culled mainly from an Akkadian source, was Utnapishtim.
This character also obtained immortality. This earliest
Noah is therefore comparable with the divine ancestor of
the Persian 'Elysium' referred to in part II of this study.

In the Gilgamesh epic no reason is given for the visit-
ation of the Flood. To quote Mr John Gray, 'Another
Akkadian myth, however, that of the Atrahasis, the Exceed-
ing Wise, which is an epithet of Utnapishtim, tells how the
gods were troubled by the rapid increase of men and the
noise they made, disturbing the peace of the gods'.

This pretext for the destruction of mankind contrasts
strangely with the arguments put forward for his creation
in an earlier Sumerian text. I quote a summary from Mr
Samuel Noah Kramer's handbook: 'After the Annunnaki,
the heaven-gods, had been born, but before the creation of
Lahar, the cattle god, and Ashnan, the grain goddess,
there existed neither cattle nor grain. The gods therefore
knew not the eating of bread nor the dressing of garments.
The cattle-god Lahar and the grain goddess Ashnan were
then created in the creation chamber of heaven, but still
the gods remained unsated. It was then that man "was
given breath", for the sake of the welfare of the sheep-
folds and the "good things" of the gods.'

In other words, man's task was regarded as providing for
the well-being and comfort of the gods, and it is hardly
likely that the latter would set about annihilating him. It
is thus evident that until the Hebrews introduced a retrib-
utory motive into the story, the Semitic versions lacked a
beginning.

When we come to consider the account of the building
of the Ark contained in the Gilgamesh version, and the
biblical version which derives from it, it becomes evident

that we have entered the realm of pure fiction. This is not
to say that all the myths referred to in this study are not
fiction of a kind. But this is deliberate novel writing, as were
most of our Parsifal sources. This is perhaps why, although
without a beginning, and in the case of the Hebrew version,
lacking the freshness and clear motivation of a Foundation
myth, these particular accounts have taken a longer lease
of the traditions of historic times, and spread wider, than
their sources.

VII

Apart from the kind of myth that pretends to explain the
origins of some striking natural phenomenon, and that
which provides an explanation for a rite of forgotten provenance, there is a species of myth that 'tells the story' of a
fragment of sculpture, or of an ikon. This myth offers the
kind of sacred or profane history that might be compiled
or collected at some time in the far distant future if, after
the destruction of our civilisation, a new and primitive
people were to colonise England, and attempt a reconstruction of our lives, and the lives of our gods, based on the
pictures still hanging behind a veil of soot and dust, in the
National Gallery.

Our first encounter with this type of myth was in the
introduction to one of Gilbert Murray's translations of
Greek plays. Long before the Aryan invasion of Greece, for
instance, some King of Aegean or Pelasgian stock lays the
foundation stone of a temple on the crown of a hill, and
the event is recorded on stone in high relief. 'What', ask
the Dorian yokels who turn this ikon up, 'was the punishment once visited upon this man' (perhaps for the crime
of belonging to a conquered or superceded people)? Their
answer was that he was condemned to pass eternity rolling

a stone to the top of a hill. At the moment of success the stone would roll down to the bottom again, and the criminal would then begin his task anew.

Mr Graves' work on the Greek Myths offers many examples of this genre of reconstruction, and though his suggestions are not capable of complete vindication, they justify themselves by a positively triumphant plausibility, particularly when we find that a particular myth has completely reversed the real and demonstrable character of an ikon. What, for instance, was the Medusa's head, which turns the beholder to stone? Well, as Mr Nelson Glueck has demonstrated in *Deities and Dolphins,* the so-called Medusa was a venerable and beneficent sea goddess whose cult was widespread throughout the Eastern Mediterranean in the first millenium B.C., and perhaps earlier.

In the course of a tour of the Aegean, Dionysus inadvertently takes passage on a pirate ship. The pirates, not knowing his true identity, decide to sell him into slavery. Dionysus transforms himself into a lion, and fills the ship with phantom animals, and the sailors, leaping overboard, are transformed into dolphins. Dionysus, Mr. Graves explains, voyaged in a new-moon boat, and the creatures with which he peopled the boat were his seasonal epiphanies. Dionysus is, in fact, Deucalion. The story of Dionysus and Deucalion was derived from an ikon. The 'launching' of the new-moon boat marks the autumnal new moon feast of Mesopotamia and Palestine, when new wine was poured out in oblation: 'the feast was celebrated on the new moon nearest to the autumnal equinox, as a means of inducing the winter rains'.

The old-fashioned ark, with its full complement of animals, that featured in the nurseries of former days, was closely related to the ark of an earlier and vanished ikon. We wonder how many traditional playthings may, in the same manner, be the progenitors of their own legend.

Dionysus mounted on a panther preceded by celebrants and followed by Silenus. The bare boughs and the tragic masks suspended from them suggest that this scene illustrates the ritual of carrying Death out of the town, in this case perhaps represented by Pentheus ("Grief") whose puppet (because he was never a living person) would have been torn to pieces.

(see "The Wild Hunt")

Painting, 18th Century, from an unknown vase. Author's collection.

left. **Stone group of Shiva with an Apsaras, the Indian counterpart of Dionysus and the Bacchantes. Central Indian mediaeval period.** (see ''The Wild Hunt'') *and above*. **A bronze Totemic deer. Provenance unknown, perhaps Northern European.** (see ''Totemism Ancient and Modern'').

Author's collection

THE WILD HUNT

Some Reflections on a Simple Legend

For the sound of his horn brought me from my bed,
And the cry of the hounds that he oft-times led,
And his loud 'View hallo' would AWAKEN THE DEAD
And the fox from his lair in the morning.

John Peel

If ye have eaten dead things and made living ones, what will
ye make if ye eat living things?
   Hippolytus, *Philosophumena* (Supposedly extracted from
     the Phrygian Mysteries)

They came to the mouths of the River CALLICHORUS,
where we are told that DIONYSUS, son of ZEUS, when
he had left the Indians and was on his way to THEBES,
established revels, with dances in front of a cave, in which
he himself passed holy and unsmiling nights.
   Apollonius of Rhodes, *The Voyage of Argo* (Book II)

I

In Northern Europe, before the Christian conversion, the hours of darkness were haunted by forms perilous both to body and soul. Long after the acceptance of Christianity, the heathen gods stuck to their old ways, the missionaries having omitted, or disdained, to follow the example of the Buddhists in converting, or adopting, the pantheon of Asiatic deities.

Thus, almost up to our own times, the Wild Huntsman still haunted the low night sky, choosing nights of cloud and wind. In Germany he was called the Woensjager, and hunted with horse, hounds, and huntsmen. This Huntsman was Wotan himself, riding a white horse for the sun in darkness, wearing a large shovel hat and a wide cloak over his shoulders. This cloak earned him the epithet 'Hakel-Barend' or Mantel Wearing. The Mantel represented the starry heavens. A similar scarf, banderole, or veil is described, and illustrated from statuary, as worn by goddesses and their attendants in ancient Nabatea (*Deities and Dolphins* by Nelson Glueck).

The legend of the Wild Hunt is widespread, and usually, but not always, associated with Wotan, Woden, or Odin. There was, for instance, a ghostly hunter with his pack who haunted the Abbot's Way on Dartmoor. In Yorkshire the hounds were called 'Gabriel's Ratchets'. The term 'Ratchets' signifies the small section of a pack which is sent on ahead to sniff out the quarry. In packs of staghounds these are called 'Tufters'. Gabriel is the Angel of Death, and was believed to send out his ratchets to find

67

those persons who were about to die.

In England also the Wild Hunt was called Herlething, from a mythical king Herla. In France it was named Mesnie Hellequin, and was led by the Hel Huntsman. Hellequin is an early rendering of the word 'Harlequin', but we prefer at present not to be led astray by this derivation. Both in England and France the Wild Hunt was also led by Arthur. Once, in the reign of Henry II, the hunt was seen in broad daylight, in the Wye Valley. Onlookers recognised certain of their dead friends among the huntsmen.

One famous variant of the genre is Herne the Hunter, who hunts in Windsor Park. Like Shiva, Herne was a wearer of horns.

Allied to the story of the Wild Hunt is the tradition of sleeping hosts who waken at night and ride across the countryside. These were led by Wotan or Arthur, or on occasion by women. The latter, in Northern Europe, included Morgan Le Fay and Dame Holle.

II

The Vedic hymns were the property, and the product, of the Aryan peoples that invaded India, entering through the Northern or Western passes early in the second millenium B.C., perhaps at the same time as the so-called Battle-axe people were invading North-eastern Europe and the British Isles: the hymns themselves took the form with which we are familiar now during the latter part of the second millenium B.C. and were written down during the first millenium B.C.

Long before the nomadic tribes of Central Asia formed their huge pastoral economies, the steppes were the home of small clans that lived by hunting, and probably kept to a fairly well-defined homeland, restricted thereto by the territorial claims of other clans like themselves, the jealous preservation of whose hunting rights was necessary to their existence.

Throughout the millenium that followed the close of the latest ice-epoch, the steppe-lands of Central Asia were subject to a gradual process of drying out: and this, bringing pressure on the increasing numbers those lands had to support, resulted in a movement of peoples towards the more stable areas of the South, a movement which has been recorded in middle-eastern archaeology.

During the same period the farming techniques that characterised the so-called Neolithic period, and developed in the lands bordering the Eastern Mediterranean, were being gradually carried northwards by land-seeking families. In an area that has been tentatively located north of the Black Sea these early migrant farmers probably came into contact with the hunting peoples of the steppes. It was probably the farmers that first saw the advantage of domesticating the animals that had previously been the prey of hunters and it was on the fringe of the settled homesteads that the first pastoral communities came into being, the herders themselves being initially drawn from the settled areas, though their methods and way of life subsequently became widespread throughout Central Asia.

Such communities should not be expected to originate a characteristic and homogenous culture, seeing that they were the children of peoples long settled, albeit in course of expansion. Rather they would be likely to gather several contributory strains—these derived from their parent communities, those acquired subsequently from their richer and more powerful neighbours, and those stemming from new conditions of life, with vestiges perhaps of the Mesolithic hunting culture.

So it would be quite mistaken to describe the religious ideas set forth in the earlier books of the Rig Veda as primitive, particularly as we have little idea what 'primitive' belief might have been.

For instance, the idea underlying the use of Soma, which we have touched on in the first essay of this book, is in no sense a primitive one. A hymn to Vishnu in the first book of the Rig Veda (Hymn 154) refers to him as 'him who measured out the earthly regions, who propped the highest places of congregation, thrice setting down his footsteps, widely striding'. This is the ritual of the three paces which features in the early Egyptian coronation ceremony.

The history of Yama, the Vedic King of the Dead, is treated of in Sukhumari Bhattacharji's *The Indian Theogony*, (Cambridge University Press), who says: 'In an Atharva Veda passage we have "Worship the son of Vivasvat, the gatherer of men, with oblations, he who was the first of the mortals to die, he who first entered this world" (Atharva Veda xviii:3:13). This is a very significant passage establishing that the son of Vivasvat was a mortal at first, but was the first to die and enter the other world (and become an immortal presumably) and that he then became a gatherer of the people, i.e. of departed souls; afterwards he was accorded divine honour, i.e. oblations and sacrifices. This career of the apotheosis of Yama is variously recorded in Vedic literature. "The gods and Yama were in strife over this world, Yama appropriated the power and strength of the gods; hence his name, Yama. The gods reflected, "Yama here has become what we are" (TS II:5:II). Here too it is evident that Yama had not always been an immortal like the other gods, but after some struggle with the established gods he wrested power and authority and was raised to the rank of a god.'

Thus it is shown that the first ancestor and ruler of the dead, who features in widespread Shamanistic funeral practice, was not acknowledged in Central Asian belief

70

much before the first millenium B.C. He existed, however, from early times in Egypt in the person of Osiris.

III

The Maruts are celebrated in a number of the earliest hymns of the Rig Veda.

> May the Maruts, they who give praise, the fire-tongued increasers of Rita, hear my praise. (Mandala I.44.14)

> Thou, O Agni, the first Angiras Rishi, hast become as god the king friend of the gods. After thy law the sages, active in their wisdom, were born, the Maruts with brilliant spears. (Mandala I.31.1)

> The Maruts, who possess the beauty of Agni, belong to all races of men. We implore their fierce, strong help. They are tumultuous, the sons of Rudra, clothed in rain, hot-spirited like lions, givers of rain. (Mandala III.26.5).

Agni, the spirit or god of fire, is equated with Rudra, the storm god. Rudra's sons are the Maruts, embodiments of lightning and wind. Rita is reason or order, that spirit of order so important in early Egyptian and Mesopotamian belief, who, in the person of Light revealed Truth, and of the Storm God routed the Monster of Chaos, who forever essayed to subvert the elements against the interests of man.

Sukhumari Bhattacharji, in *The Indian Theogony*, derives the name Marut from the Sanskrit 'mr' to die, a root found in modern Indian dialects, and indeed in all European tongues. This suggests that they are in reality the spirits of the dead, and this derivation reminds us of one of the basic Egyptian concepts of the after-life, that it returns the dead, in the company of their king, to the sphere of natural being, of earth, plants, and trees, of the elements and of the sea, of sun and moon and stars. They are, like Osiris himself, ex-officio guardians of the fertility of the earth.

It has been suggested that the old English Morris Dancers derived their name from the same root, and are brothers of the Maruts.

'Rudra' means 'fierce'. In the course of time, Rudra's personality and attributes became merged with those of Siva, and the latter grew to be one of the triad of great gods. The word Siva, or Sarva, is derived from 'Sara', the arrow, which illustrates both his earlier role of storm god, and his later of destroyer. The name of Rudra does not entirely die out of later writings, and 'the Rudras' are virtually co-terminal with the Maruts. The Mahabharata, a comparatively far later work, mentions Rudra as living on top of Mount Meru in the company of ghosts.

Siva is possibly the most interesting God ever assembled out of the diverse dreams and aspirations of mankind. In the course of the Aryan penetration of India he absorbed innumerable lesser tribal deities and cultic functions. In discussing some of his attributes thus accrued, together with earlier Vedic strains, we will make no attempt to present a consistent picture of a deity, or to trace logical or moral links between one function or another. He is Siva, and has India as his mother.

From Rudra he inherited the position of Lord of Animals. This ancient title may derive from the famous cave paintings of a sorcerer who wears several animal travesties at once. Certainly the Shamen of Siberia knew of a great spirit who was Lord of the Animals, and the Esquimaux believed in a Lord of the Fishes.

The familiar Indus Valley seal of a horned god squatting in a contemplative posture surrounded by animals has been regarded, with good reason, as a prototype of Siva, who is commonly depicted clothed in animal skins and seated on one. Evidently, in an unhappily familiar sacerdotal manner, the Shaman of past history, from being nothing more than an intermediary with this guardian both of beasts and of hunters, eventually took his entire role on himself.

His sacred animal is the bull, the universal Asiatic emblem of physical power and potency: and he was also worshipped in the form of a phallus, particularly in southern India, where the Savaitic faith still has strongest hold.

He was both austere and profligate, meditative and drunken. These antinomies would have broken any but a universal character; it would be well, at this point, to consider them further, and separately.

Such is the malicious envy with which, in the view of many simple peoples, the dead regard the living, that to be happy may expose a person to 'spiritual danger' (how easily, in the study of anthropology, one trips over terms and technicalities familiar in European nineteenth and twentieth-century theology). Thus the safest way of life on earth is that of poverty and humility. From this conclusion it is a short step to the idea that, by the exercise of sufficiently dire and prolonged mortification, an ascetic may establish a legitimate claim on the consideration of the dead, and even some degree of power over them. The calculable response of the Gods is, in this respect, identified with that of the dead. (We have drawn the argument from Briffault's *Reasons for Anger*). Asceticism has, however, a Shamanistic provenance also. In familiar Shamanistic practice, a Shaman pursues his great journeys into the realm of the spirit by means of ecstatic stimulation, in the form of drumming, singing, and dancing. In more sophisticated times and locales, the journey becomes one of ritual or thought.

'The Brahmanic sacrifice,' says Mircea Eliade in *Shamanism,* 'mounts to heaven by ritually climbing a ladder'.

(This is the way of symbolism, or sympathetic magic.) 'The Buddhist Yogi through meditation, realises an ascent whose nature is completely spiritual.'

But Buddhism, of course, was a late off-shoot of Brahmanism. Siva was before Buddha, and the method of liberating the spirit by meditation was a Hindu technique. The Yogi can fly through space, but only because he has liberated himself by the exercise of concentrated thought.

'Siva', says the *Classical Dictionary of Hindu Mythology*, (by John Dawson, Trubner's Oriental Series, Routledge & Kegan Paul) 'is the Maha-Yogi, the great ascetic, in whom is centred the highest perfection of austere penance and abstract meditation, by which the most unlimited powers are attained, marvels and miracles are worked, the highest spiritual knowledge is acquired, and union with the great spirit of the universe is eventually gained. In this character he is the naked ascetic Dig-Ambara, "clothed with the elements", or Dhur-Jati, "loaded with matted hair", and his body smeared with ashes'.

It is worth noting that in Siva we have a classic example of a Hero, but with a very special life history, one which reflects the unique genius of Indian thought, religion, and history, and no mere ritual champion of his people, like Horus, Hercules, or Arthur. Even here, however, there are echoes. He fought and killed a dragon (in fact an elephant-demon), and both Rudra's son Skanda, and Siva's son Karttikeya, were born among bull-rushes.

It is a perfectly legitimate deduction from world mythology that any god who performs the functions of a mediator (e.g. an ascetic or Yogi), or is frequently reincarnated, is not, in origin, a true god, but is a priest or king, or both, just as the historic Gautama Buddha was born to be a king, but repudiated his divine ancestry. Few individuals of this genre, however, have become historically established, perhaps because their dynasty or succession flourished in pre-literate times. None outside Asia has bequeathed to humanity a 'revealed' philosophy (that is to say, a philosophy of legitimate and sacerdotal source): and it is to Hinduism that we owe the cardinal doctrine of Buddhism, that of non-attachment, though Buddha added the Middle Way, expressed by T. S. Eliot as 'to care and not to care'. To Hinduism also we are indebted for the teaching of Karma, the inevitable progress of the soul through many incarnations, determined by the actions of that soul, an esoteric concept which might have saved the Christian Church, had the latter seen fit to adopt it, from less plausible means and destinies. It is noteworthy that Siva, in his later icons, is depicted wearing the crescent of the moon, thus associating him with death and reincarnation.

A very different kind of association, however, is related of Siva in the Mahabharata. Here he is described as the leader of a retinue of grisly monsters, seeming to resemble creatures out of a fantasy by Hieronymous Bosch. These make merry in the manner of a witches' Sabbath, devour raw flesh and drink blood. They are evidently supernatural monsters, or ghosts belonging to a somewhat elementary stage of savage belief. Some idea of the mentality that evokes this most disturbing and unedifying concept of the dead can be glimpsed from a horizon of cave relief carving that is found at many sites in Spain, and has been illustrated in *The Rock Pictures of Europe*. Many primitive people even now will draw a 'spirit' in such terms, as witness the Esquimau in *The World of the Early Hunters* who is recorded as having so terrified himself by his impromptu bit of reportage that he had to go to his tent and hide. In keeping with his leadership of this rout, Siva bears the designations of Bhutanatha and Pramatheca, lord of ghosts and spirits. In time, however, these creatures were depicted as resembling Siva himself.

In considering the aggregate of characteristics that makes

Siva's character, we encounter a catholicity of religious outlook that easily dies out of the religion of an orderly and sophisticated society such as ours. Rudra is given homage in the Satarudriya hymns in the Yajurveda as the patron of criminals and outlaws, of what our own civilisation has learned to regard as positively evil. Yet the idea, in its practical working out, is not far removed from the inner bearing of the Biblical Book of Job. Is death itself an evil? And, if not, is a murderer totally evil? Is theft altogether wicked? Then are riches to be regarded as an unalloyed good? Job, in Indian theological terms, was working out an almost blameless Karma, throughout circumstances that arose from the caprices of nature and human life. We are not told of the Karma of the robbers themselves. When Indians give praise to the god of the robbers, they are portraying themselves as the world's total theists. There is a God everywhere and in everything, and the universal god comprehends the multitude. When an Indian is stricken with smallpox, he can offer prayers and sacrifices to the God or Goddess of Smallpox. It is better than to be delivered over to a devil, or anarchy, or the staff of an isolation hospital.

When Siva went hunting with his macabre pack, he was, in one aspect, herding souls along the paths of Metempsychosis. He was, however, also performing the functions of the destroyer who consumes to regenerate. Flesh and blood are needed to sustain the harvests of the coming year. The Aztec fields were sprinkled with blood to help them produce crops. The dead, the agents of growth, must consume life in order to stimulate life.

Siva is shown in certain ikons as a sleeping figure upon whose recumbent body dances Kali, his Shakti and the goddess of death and life. Dancing is a magic rite that encourages the dance of animals and birds, leaping salmon and waving crops. Therefore the host of Siva danced on their predatory errand. Even in present-day India, says Mr Sukumari Bhattarcharji, many cults are connected with intoxication, and intoxication is the magical life-blood of a god who dies, is consumed, and is re-born.

In concluding this brief section on the Wild Hunt in ancient India, which leads us from the Vedic age, through the Brahmanic and Puranic to the full flowering of Hinduism, it is well to utter a caution against the temptation to assume too readily that we have been witnessing the metamorphosis of an idea from simple, clean, and chivalric origins, through a decline wrought by the decadent influence of an aboriginal native populace, first conquered and then absorbed, to its final debasement in the atmosphere of Tantrism. To be sure, a powerful factor in the growth and formulation of Tantric concepts was an urge to revitalise the life of a religion too easily dominated by abstractions and ideals of mortification. But we know hardly anything of the actual life and behaviour of the Aryan invaders, or indeed of the ways of the inhabitants of India of those days. Mr. Mircea Eliade, in his great work on Yoga, notes that 'it is difficult to separate the Indo-European contribution from the post-Aryan substratum.' And 'At the time of their arrival in India, the Indo-Europeans also preserved a number of archaic cultural elements'.

Thus we should not be too surprised to note that a variant of the Wild Hunt flourishes to this day among the simple Tamil villagers of Southern India. It is described at length in Stella Kramrisch's essay 'Indian Varieties of Art Ritual', which has been published in *Myths and Symbols: Studies in Honour of Mircea Eliade* (Kitagawa and Long). It is associated with the cult of Aiyanar, whom a late 'myth of assimilation' (described by the author as 'artificial syncretism') makes the son of Siva out of Vishnu in the shape of a woman Mohini—a truly monstrous example of priestly chicanery.

'In some of his sanctuaries', says Miss Kramrisch, 'Aiya-nar is represented in human shape; a kingly equestrian figure, he rides on a horse or an elephant. Horses are offered to him, large terra-cotta horses so that he does not lack a mount during the watches of the night when he rides aroung the village and looks after its safety. He rides with his retinue of heroes—and demons. Two horses at least must be offered to Aiyanar each year. The second is for Karuppan, the "dark god", the demon who accompanies him. Over the years, the horses accumulate in a sacred grove. Up to five hundred such large clay horses (twelve feet or more high) may be ready in one sanctuary for the nocturnal rides. New horses are set up while the old and broken ones are left to decay and return to the earth of which they were made. Under the image of Aiya-nar a stone linga, the phallic symbol of Siva's creativeness, is buried. The seed of Siva, from which Aiyanar was born, it is said, fell near the bank of the waters.'

Later, the author says, 'The main sanctuary of Aiyanar, the Lord, is in the thickly wooded Shabari Hills in Kerala near the western coast of South India. There the Lord protects man from evil spirits and endows him with knowledge which leads to salvation. But in the sanctuary of Erumeli in Kerala, Aiyanar is worshipped in the form of a hunter. His devotees dance wildly when they worship the Lord of this world of delusion, might, and fear'. And further, 'The Lord, Aiyanar, the guardian of the land, has his generals and lieutenants. They are heroes (vira), that is, the souls of those who died in battle. They are joined by the host of demons, of which the foremost is Karuppan, the dark god, who is all that Aiyanar is not. He is the adversary to whom blood sacrifices are due. Aiyanar is worshipped with flowers and fruits. The dark power within Aiyanar, the Hunter, has been hypostatized into Karuppan, his alter ego, the demon as protector'.

It is reasonable to assume that the 'blood sacrifices' mentioned in the latter extract refer to the ancient Aryan horse sacrifice. Whether the horse was associated with the rite ab origine is not known, nor whether the sacrifice was ever more than a symbolic creature of clay. Alternatively, the sacrifice could have been the object of a ritual hunt.

IV

'There were in the Indo-Iranian language three words expressive of divinity: Asura, "the Lord", Yagata, "the one who is worthy of sacrifice, Daeva, "the shining one". Asura became the name of the supreme God, Yagata was the general name of all gods. Now as there were old Indo-Iranian formulae which deprecated the wrath of both men and devas (gods), or invoked the aid of some god against the hate and oppression of both men and devas, that word daeva which had become obsolete (because Asura and Yagata met all the wants of religious language) took by and by from formulae of this kind a dark and fiendish meaning. What favoured the change was the want of a technical word for expressing the general notion of a fiend, a want the more felt as the dualistic idea acquired greater strength and distinction.'

This passage, from Chapter IV of James Darmesteter's Introduction to the *Zend Avesta,* is of notable interest as providing an instance of religious thought in decline, a subject naturally enough avoided or ignored by religious establishments in all ages. The Persian religion, of course, grew up on this definitive embodiment of the idea of an absolute good opposed by an absolute evil. Health and life were opposed by sickness and decay, good thought was reflected in evil thought, 'Savru, the arrow of death' (a name derived from the same root as Siva), 'Indra, a name or epithet of fire as destructive . . . became the demons of tyranny, corruption, and impiety.'

Thus an attempt to purify the gods lead inevitably to their weakening. In the old Germanic religion, the powers of evil were eventually triumphant, and brought the reign of the enfeebled gods to an end, or at least to the end of an age. In what one is justified in calling the Mesopotamian complex of religions, evil, the work of devils, is allowed to prosper for a time, although it is finally brought to book by means of an universal purgation, in which the 'sheep' are separated from the 'goats'. But the tainted universe has got to be destroyed and remade. It is true that in the moralistic thought of our age casuistry has largely taken the place of explicit law, and it is permissible to particularise Good and Evil by the motives that prompt the commission itself, by the maturity, judgement and understanding of the agent. It can be observed, however, that few religious teachers are able for long to resist the temptation to discharge broadsides at 'naked evil', or even 'evil in disguise', and the attitude has furthermore cast its black and rigid shadow on the issues of politics, so much so that we can claim with justice that moral dualism is the chief materialiser of extreme political wings, whose actual policies are notoriously equivocal.

The fissure that we have watched appear in ancient religious unities has now broken the unity of Rudra, and his spirit host. Still quoting the same commentary in the *Zend Avesta,* 'Then came the host of storm fiends, the Drvants, the Dvarants, the Dregvants, all names meaning 'the running ones', and referring to the headlong course of the fiends in storm, 'the onsets of the wounding crew'. One of the foremost among the Drvants, their leader in their onsets, is Aeshma, 'the raving', 'a fiend with the wounding spear'. Originally a mere epithet of the storm fiend, Aeshma was afterwards converted into an abstract, the demon of rage and anger, and became an expression for all moral wickedness, a mere name of Ahriman'. Virtually synonymous with these Drvants are the Daevas, to which we have referred above which became 'the fiends who assail the sky'.

V

No apology need be offered for citing the following example of a Ritual Hunt of peculiarly Egyptian complexion. It is abstracted from *Egyptian Religion* by Sir Wallis Budge.

> There is no reason for doubting the antiquity of the Egyptian belief in the resurrection of the dead and in immortality, and the general evidence derived both from archaeological and religious considerations supports this view. As old, however, as this belief in general is the specific belief in a spiritual body (Sah or Sahu); for we find it in texts of the Vth dynasty incorporated with ideas which belong to the pre-historic Egyptian in his savage or semi-savage state. One remarkable extract will prove this point. In the funeral chapters which are inscribed on the walls of the chambers and passages inside the pyramid of King Unas, who flourished at the end of the Vth dynasty, about B.C. 3300, is a passage in which the deceased king terrifies all the powers of heaven and earth because he 'riseth as a soul (Ba) in the form of the god who liveth upon his fathers and who maketh food of his mothers. Unas is the lord of wisdom and his mother knoweth not his name. He hath become mighty like unto the god Temu, the father who gave him birth, and after Temu gave him birth he became stronger than his father.' The king is likened unto a Bull, and he feedeth upon every god, whatever may be the

81

form in which he appeareth; 'he hath weighed words with the god whose name is hidden,' and he devoureth men and liveth upon gods. The dead king is then said to set out to hunt the gods in their meadows, and when he has caught them with nooses, he causes them to be slain. They are next cooked in blazing cauldrons, the greatest for his morning meal, the lesser for his evening meal, and the least for his midnight meal; the old gods and goddesses serve as fuel for his cooking pots. In this way, having swallowed the magical powers and spirits of the gods, he becomes the Great Power of Powers among the gods, and the greatest of the gods who appear in visible forms. 'Whatever he hath found upon his path he hath consumed, and his strength is greater than that of any spiritual body (Sahu) in the horizon; he is the firstborn of all the firstborn, and . . . he hath carried off the hearts of the gods . . . He hath eaten the wisdom of every god, and his period of existence is everlasting, and his life shall be unto all eternity . . . for the souls and the spirits of the gods are in him.'

We have, it is clear, in this passage an allusion to the custom of savages of all nations and periods, of eating portions of the bodies of valiant foes whom they have vanquished in war in order to absorb their virtues and strength; the same habit has also obtained in some places in respect of animals. In the case of the gods the deceased is made to covet their one peculiar attribute, that is to say, everlasting life; and when he has absorbed their souls and spirits he is declared to have obtained all that makes him superior to every other spiritual body in strength and in length of life. The 'magical powers' (heka), which the king is also said to have 'eaten', are the words and formulae, the utterance of which by him, in whatever circumstances he may be placed, will cause every being, friendly or unfriendly, to do his will.

Dionysus is spoken of in Homer, and the festivals in which his cult was celebrated in classical times were of undetermined antiquity. The fact that his image was carried in procession in a wheeled ship has been taken as evidence that his cult arrived in Greece by sea, which is as much as to say that the cult of Father Christmas arrived in Northern Europe by air. We have referred briefly to the ship association of Dionysus in our essay on the Flood. Classical Greece regarded Thrace as a possibly early venue of his cult and the Thracians may have arrived in Greece about 1000 B.C.

Dionysus was a God inter-alia of wine, but he had also many vegetative connections, particularly ivy, an evergreen which has a particular addiction to churchyards, the pine, a symbol throughout Asia of age and longevity, and the fig, a fruit in which the ancients perceived sexual connotations, perhaps because, like the pomegranate, it is packed with tiny seeds. Fig wood was used for the carving of phalli, and the fig was also sacred to Priapus. Ivy could be used to 'send' devotees into trances. The myrtle was also symbolic of Dionysus and of the dead.

It is noteworthy that Dionysus was not in the fullest sense a Corn God, although one story tells of his cradle as a winnowing basket. His celebration in music and dance admittedly endowed him and his followers with the power to stimulate fertility, but it was perhaps a human and animal fertility. All nature dances, the trees in the fecundating wind, the young of animals, the child in the womb: and periodic orgies, punctuating the grim life of poor subsistence economies, were accompanied by sexual licence.

Dionysus possessed many animal avatars, notably the bull; his affinity lay with animals, and at the same time he was required to assure his mastery over animals, and in this respect he symbolised the situation of the early hunter.

As 'Lord of the Animals' he and his followers or maenads were reputed to hunt wild animals and devour them raw: they were also said to practice child stealing and cannibalism. We can surely equate this with ritual hunting, as for instance the hunting of the wren in Northern Europe in historical times, but the hunt of Dionysus had the wider object of vivifying the God and his host with flesh and blood.

The 'madness' of Dionysus has received some attention in semi-mystical studies of his legend. Followers of Siva were sometimes similarly described as 'lunatics'. But we can safely accept that they were not cretins, nor subject to demens praecox or degenerative conditions, and their progress was not the effect of locomotus ataxus. The term 'madness' merely indicates that they behaved, on ritual occasions, wildly, like Wotan or Woden, 'the wild one'.

Dionysus was a god of the Dead. He grew up in the house of Persephone, as the Orphic hymns testify, and was believed to sleep in the house of Persephone in between his reincarnations or resurrections—probably a reference to the dark of the moon. At the festival of the Anthesteria, to which we referred in the essay on the Flood, the entry into Athens of Dionysus in his ship occurred simultaneously with the return of the dead to their old homes. The Agrionia was a festival of the dead, and in certain parts of Greece the celebrants made a search for Dionysus who had 'disappeared', like the Suffering God of Babylonia and the Keeper of the Holy Grail, the supplanted king. The Maenads were liable to be overtaken, in the midst of their revels, by a frozen silence—Walter Otto in *Dionysus, Myth and Cult,* terms it the 'sombre madness', and in this act believes them to be identifying themselves with the spirits of the dead. Dionysus is much portrayed iconographically as a mask, and a mask is employed widely throughout the barbaric world as a means of identifying a person with his ancestors, or with ghosts generally.

Similarly, perhaps, the priests of Siva still daub their faces heavily with ashes, in honour of the god of the funeral pyre, and of his early identification, as Rudra, with Agni, the spirit of life and the consumer of the dead.

Mr. Nelson Glueck, in *Deities and Dolphins,* makes a most interesting observation on the uses of the mask in the iconography of the region of his study. 'The Nabataean use of the tragic mask furnishes yet another example of their preoccupation with immortality and their intense desire to become identified with divinity.' (This 'identification with divinity' could well serve as a definition of religion in its widest sense, understood, perhaps, as identification in life also, and not only in death.) 'The use of the tragic mask suggesting the face of death was another means to the same end of achieving immortal status. The mask served as a portrait of the deathless god, of Dushara, Dusares, Dionysus, and its wearer became united with him through its use for life everlasting, escaping thus the limitations of the mortal span.' It would be tempting to suggest—much as we prefer evidence to speculation, however ingenious—that the tragic mask corresponded to what Catholics refer to as the Church Militant, and the mask of comedy represented the concept of the Church Triumphant.

Thus we have to consider Dionysus in the role of Mediator and Saviour. One of his epithets was 'Deliverer', and he possessed the power of liberating himself and his followers when they had been thrown into chains.

To complete what should now be a somewhat familiar portrait, it should be noted that Dionysus was the son of a mortal mother, Semele: his disposal at birth was eccentric— he was washed up on the shore of Laconia in a chest together with his mother,—he was a triumphant conqueror, he taught his people the arts of civilisation, he was killed violently at Thebes, and one of his tombs at least was at Delphi. Thus he was a typical Hero: and Sir James Frazer identified his legend tentatively with the history of a dynasty of Dying Kings, although it would be more pertinent,—and the documentary evidence is more authentic,—to compare his story with that of Horus.

The resemblances between the cults of Dionysus and Siva are so numerous that one is justified in claiming that they are one and the same god, contaminated however in different ways by drawing into themselves the cults of widely separated regions. Siva has endured, and gained in strength and stature. Dionysus has disappeared, his role of Redeemer absorbed into a religion of monistic and platonic complexion that was ready to destroy the phenomenal world for the sake of moral simplification. Many feel that the Indians have preserved the only truly catholic worship. However, theology is not the immediate concern of this essay.

Both Dionysus and Siva were revered in phallic form: and that the true significance of this observance should be appreciated, (and how far it is from the anthropology of Cold Comfort Farm), we will close this section by quoting some paragraphs of Lewis Richard Farnell's *Greek Hero Cults and Ideas of Immortality* (pp. 356-7).

> That the ancestral spirits fostered the life of each new generation is the idea expressed by the offerings brought to them on the occasion of marriage. Was this belief ever developed in Greece into a doctrine of palingenesis, that the soul of the ancestor might be re-born in a new incarnation? We find this dimly recorded of the old Thraco-Phrygian religion, and it is worked up in the Orphic doctrine that descends from that source. It may explain the consecration of the stone-phallus that appears on the prehistoric Phrygian tumuli; the naive naturalism of primitive thought expressing thus in the clearest fashion the faith that death was the source of new life, the ghost the procreator of a new birth.

We can discover sporadic traces of the same expression of the same idea in Greece. The mound near Megalopolis, with a pillar upon it shaped like a finger and called 'Finger'—and explained by a story of Orestes biting off his finger in his madness, may be interpreted as a tumulus crowned with a phallus, and it is associated with the goddess called the Maniai, whose name arouses the suspicion of a Phrygian origin. Again, the legend of Dionysus and Prosymnos, stripped of the obscene mythology that has gathered round it, clearly points to the same practice. Finally, clinching evidence has been supplied by the discovery of an inscription found under a stone-phallus on a small hill that may have been a tumulus near Thespiai, recording a dedication by the religious officials of the State 'to the spirits of the dead'. Other examples might be found of this interesting monumental custom that throws light on the soul-theory of a dark period concerning which literature is silent. We may surmise that the same idea explains the Attic custom of burying the dead person with his face turned towards the east and of giving to the new-born child the name of its deceased grandfather.

VII

The researches so briefly summarised belong to the field of early history: the term 'anthropology' would not be appropriate, since it implies that the ideas we have been studying have grown out of man and his conditions as naturally as his skin or hair: that they are the proper and inevitable things for men to believe and practise, that they evolved from something simple into something more elaborate,—and that all people practised them. On the contrary, none of the information available to us, but for the inconclusive evidence of a few figurines or cave paintings, goes any further back in time than the earliest extant documents, and the contemporary conditions and the living memories they record.

In composing this 'introduction' to a vast subject—because the studies contained herein enshrine a vast subject—we have mentioned evidence only from early Indian, Persian, Middle Eastern, Greek, and Teutonic traditions. We have not considered ancient American testimony, for instance, although this is not lacking: in *Mexican and Central American Mythology* by Irene Nicholson, the following passage occurs: 'For example, there was a herb called petum with analgesic properties if used as an ointment on the skin. Used in combination with an hallucinogen, and by a man unable to distinguish between power and cruelty on the one hand, and power allied to virtue on the other, petum could become a sinister instrument. A Spanish chronicler called Acosta described how: " . . . by means of this ointment they became witches, and saw and spoke to the devil. The priests, when smeared with this ointment, lost all fear, and became imbued with cruelty. So they boldly killed men in their sacrifices, going all alone at night to the mountains, and into dark caves, not fearing any wild beasts because they were sure that lions, tigers, snakes and other savage animals that breed in the mountains and forests would flee from them because of this petum of their god . . . This petum also served to cure the sick, and for children; and so they called it the divine remedy . . . so the people went to the priests and holy men, who encouraged the blind and ignorant in this error, persuading them what they pleased and making them pursue their inventions and diabolical ceremonies . . . "'

On page 241 of the same study (according to the page numbers of the triple volume, *Mythology of the Americas*) there is a picture of Tlacolteutl, the earth and fertility goddess, riding on a broomstick. Here we may remind readers that Margaret Murray, the authority on European witch cults, drew a comparison between the celebrations of these cults and those of the Bacchic maenads, even to the uttering of the cry 'A boy, a boy', which she thought might have been a corruption of the Greek 'Evoe'. Sir James Frazer in *The Golden Bough* deals exhaustively with the significance of the broom, the 'storm besom', connected through the mistletoe with the night riding of the powers of wind, thunder, and lightning, in fact of the 'Rudras'.

The two most fertile sources of reference material are India and Greece. These provide illustrations of somewhat confused and complex religious systems, having many points of mutual resemblance, and some characteristic modifications or differences. A conquering cult will doubtless draw to it many lesser and local cults, and these would account for the differences. Complexes of belief or practice which are held in common, however, have some claim to be regarded as primary, as forming one system from the beginning. We have referred earlier to the close relationship between cults of nature and cults of the dead. (Why, incidentally, must every writer on anthropology invariably refer to Nature as 'Fertility'?) These were, in the customs we are studying, conjoined in the person of a minor God, or his regent, or of a hero, or divine king, or line of divine kings. With him the subject or follower was united at death, and with him perhaps he entered into the cosmic life. In their lifetime, ritual hunting was the sport of kings: after their translation, perhaps they were thought of as hunters of men, although in practice there was no such ritual as far as we know.

Backward peoples are prone to take advanced peoples as their models: discarded manners or fashions pass to what are now termed 'underprivileged classes', or to peoples peripheral to the established civilisations.

These manners may return to their progenitors at times of decline, and may themselves have in the meantime lost some of their original meaning, or declined into barbarism. Let us give an example. The importance of the principle merits quotation at length. It is from Irene Nicholson's *Mexican and Central American Mythology,* from which we have already given an extract, pp. 202 & 203.

The Nahua peoples believed that we are born with a physical heart and face, but that we have to create a deified heart and a true face. The ordinary word for heart was yollotl, a word derived from ollin, movement. Thus the ordinary human heart is the moving, pumping organ that keeps us alive; but the heart that can be made by special efforts in life is called Yolteotl, or deified. The phrase used to describe the face that we must make if we are to be truly men is ixtli in yollotl, which signifies a process whereby heart and face must combine. The heart must shine through the face before our features become reliable reflections of ourselves.

Thus heart-making and face-making, the growth of spiritual strength, were two aspects of a single process which was the aim of life and which consisted in creating some firm and enduring centre from which it would be possible to operate as human beings. Without this enduring centre, as the Nahua poet tells us:

> . . . you give your heart to each thing in turn.
> Carrying, you do not carry it.
> You destroy your heart on earth.
> Are you not always pursuing things idly?

If we are unable to create this second heart and face, we are merely vagrants on the face of the earth. The idea of vagrancy is expressed in the word ahuicpa, which means literally 'to carry something untowardly' or without direction. There is another word, itlatiuh, which means to pursue things aimlessly. Ahuicpa tic huica means 'carrying, you do not carry it'—and this directionless carrying was believed by the Nahuas to be typical of man's ordinary state on earth. By accident we do not achieve direction, any more than we can be sure of travelling from London to Edinburgh by going to a station booking office and asking for the first ticket that comes to hand, or by thoughtlessly boarding the first bus that comes along because it happens to be moving.

But of course this idea of feeding the sun with a symbolic heart, created within a man's psyche, was very soon distorted. Offerings to the gods made in flowers picked from the meadows and the cornfields became offerings of enemy hearts torn out. As the friar Bernardino de Sahagun tells us: 'They used to make the prisoner climb on to the stone, which was round like a millstone. And when the captive was on the stone one of the priests . . . took a rope, which went through the eyelet of the millstone, and bound him by the waist. Then he gave him a wooden sword, which instead of knives had bird feathers stuck to the edge; and gave him four pine staves with which to defend himself and overthrow his adversary.'

In this way the prisoners were made to fight and kill one another, or alternatively the hearts were torn out by their captors. Either way it was the end of them, and the sun was left metaphorically licking its chops.

The whole gory process is a long way from the Nahua ideal of creating the heart Yolteotl, or of the Maya idea described by a modern student Domingo Martinez Paredez: 'One god who gave life and consciousness, and another who fashioned him, that is, who not only gave consciousness to man but at the same time formed and gave him human shape: only he had the virtue of being able to raise man above the other animals. So in Maya anthropogeny there exists the concept not only that consciousness is given to man, but also that it must be formed, and it is the gods' task to do this'.

Historically speaking, we associate this characteristic 'loss of culture' with the coming of the Aztecs, formerly a peripheral race of barbarians.

In the same way, history permits us to wonder whether the bloody rites of Dionysus might not have been an exaggeration or literalisation of an occasional or periodic act of ritual hunting performed by the ministers of a higher civilisation.

For instance, 'bull leaping' was practised in Minoan Crete: frescoes of an earlier date from Anatolia, the cradle of Neolithic civilisation, illustrate the same custom. This ritual seems to have had the object of establishing the power of man as ascendent over the greatest power in nature: iconographic evidence suggests that the bull was driven into a net, so that it could be ritually sacrificed as a surrogate of the 'dying god'. This ritual, as we know, declined in our era into a sport which involved holocausts of bulls.

So vast is the difference in time between the date of the earliest decipherable records, and that of our first full experience of the life of savages (as, for instance, in the course of the exploration of equatorial Africa), that it is patently unsound to draw historical conclusions from the later evidence that cannot be confirmed from the earlier. For instance, cannibalism as a social practice has been regarded with abhorrence in all literate ages. Yet anthropologists assume without question that it was a familiar feature of the life of primitive man. But where is their evidence? Could it not have been adopted as a result of a misinterpretation of some civilised ritual, such as the eating of the body of a god in the form of wheaten cakes?

There is a familiar Egyptian legend to the effect that the body of Osiris was chopped into small fragments, and that Isis collected the pieces for burial. Sir James Frazer has cited a number of 'fertility' customs from various parts of the world that show that this story has been in fact translated into practice. Perhaps: but what of the original legend itself? Later scholarship proposes that it was an etiological myth, suggested by the large numbers of cult sites and tombs of Osiris scattered through Egypt. Angelo Brelish, in *Symbol of a Symbol* (from *Myths and Symbols: Studies in Honour of Mercea Eliade*; Kitagawa and Long) says, 'It is known that while human sacrifices were very rare in ancient Greece, they recur in an enormous number of Greek myths. This singular discrepancy between ritual praxis and myth is generally interpreted in the sense that myths would retain the memories of a more ancient epoch wherein human sacrifices were conducted more frequently. On the basis of extant documents, however, one would have difficulties in exactly identifying this epoch: certainly, it was not the Mycenaean, for which neither texts, representations, nor results of excavations furnish any documentary evidence. To claim that we may refer to an even older epoch would be gratuitous and also unlikely: the Greek myths, which speak of human sacrifices, reflect religious and cultural conditions quite different from those of the Middle or Early Helladic Period'.

This quotation brings us back to the myth of Dionysus. It prompts the suggestion that the bloody element in the rites attendant on his worship may have been practised by some savage peripheral tribe, such as the Thracians, in exaggeration of a far more restrained and hieratic type of ritual hunt: that is to say, if they were ever practised at all.

VIII

We have not read 'Hunting as a Ceremony of State: a review of the Royal Sport from earliest recorded times'. Probably it has not been written: perhaps some such title could be found among those massive treatises of the 19th century that made their way into the statutary libraries in greater numbers than ever came out.

We know that hunting in historic times was conducted in a manner deserving of the adjective 'ritualistic'. The officers of various rank and function, the uniforms, the score books of meaningful horn calls, well described in Sir Sacheverall Sitwell's *The Hunters and the Hunted,* the solemn blooding of novices at the kill, the distribution and preservation of the relics, all lend dignity to a pursuit that, even now, when its objective is 'The Thief of the World', is regarded as worthy of a great civilisation.

The sport has not, generally, been pursued in a condition of drunkenness. The writer has, incidentally, always approached Euripides' description of the Wild Hunt in the Bacchae with a modicum of scepticism. How far can drunken people run on steep hillsides? Would they really be any match for the sober denizens of the forest? Would they be inspired by the rhapsodical fervour expressed in such incomparable language by Euripides, language which Sir Gilbert Murray understood to convey the innermost feelings of Euripides in regard to poetry itself?

The few Englishmen who still survive to pursue this sport 'in the heavy shires', where 'greyness is on the fields, and sunset like a line of pagan pyres' certainly enjoy their pleasures more soberly, at greater length, more truly and profoundly than a Thracian—or could it have been a Celtic —barbarian. The English, be it remembered, invented football. The 'supporters' of Lancashire and Glasgow destroyed it.

Hunting is the sport of kings, and, in ancient times, of divine kings, many of whom bore the names of 'legendary' god ancestors, such as Dionysus or Herakles, perhaps themselves only lines drawn into infinity from the names of the dynasties that re-enacted their labours.

The Saxon kings that invaded Britain claimed descent from Wotan. The fact that Arthur was associated with a Wild Hunt suggests that he also could have claimed descent from Wotan. The idea is formulated, to be immediately relinquished. Nothing whatever is known of a historic Arthur, but his associations in legend do appear to be Celtic of the pagan period: not only is the Wild Hunt itself a pagan vestige, but many circumstances closely and constantly related to Arthur's story, for instance the practice of taking heads in ambush or battle, or 'headhunting', could not possibly apply to the Christian Romano-Celtic period. We know that pagan Teutonic tribes, for instance the Franks, took heads. It may be that roots of the Arthurian legend reach yet deeper into time, into the Bronze Age, when it is thought that a homogenous culture of royal and aristocratic complexion may have embraced the greater part of Europe, and when perhaps contact with the ancient civilisations of the Mediterranean was freer than in the Iron Age. All these questions lie in the shadow of the true Dark Ages, the ages wherein Archaeology is the only History, at least in the North.

IX

Archaeology is the silent complement to History, and cannot be treated by the comparative method, by type rather than by period. It belongs to the sphere of history and not of the abstract human studies, whether these be plausibly demonstrable or merely speculative.

Pre-history is also a branch of History, and not of any kind of natural law. Observations in the fields of mythology, sociology, or so-called anthropology,—rather too wide a term, comprising a boundless tract of classes—belong initially to the period in which they are, or were, recorded. They, too, are a part of human history, but the chronological element in this is the great disputed factor. Nobody now credits the earlier concept of the existence of associated groups of racial, lingual, and cultural features. The process of diffusion (the diffusion of the garments of human life, and not of its flesh) is still little understood, though Sir Mortimer Wheeler has shed a strange light on the question in his essay *Archaeology and the Transmission of Ideas*. He says 'there is every sort of mystery in the thought of the transmission of a *disembodied* idea of writing from the Euphrates to the Indus'. But there is a possible explanation of this. At the stage of culture at which his 'idea' could have been passed, it is not unlikely that an objection was felt to the communication of the actual symbols in which the names of the gods, kings, cities, etc., were recorded in the parent country, seeing that these could be used by an enemy to effect injury in the magical sense. It is well known, however, that such commodities as songs and dances are traded between neighbouring tribes, and "backward" peoples are always eager to find out what factors, techniques, or secrets have given stronger neighbours their superiority. The processes of diffusion seem to go from the richer to the poorer, the stronger to the weaker, the wiser to the simpler: in the process there will, of course, be distortion, and a lowering of 'civilised standards'.

TOTEMISM ANCIENT AND MODERN

Curiously enough, it is only more or less dangerous beasts
that men choose to become: the lion, leopard, hyena, wild
dog, elephant, a snake, and the fabulous Itoshi monster.
Sometimes a person may choose to become all the first four
or five of these. A doctor provides the necessary medicine . . .
Lucien Levy-Bruhl,   *The 'Soul' of the Primitive* (quoting)

'O Holy Thoth, the true sight of whose face none of the
Gods endures, make me to be in every creature's true form—
wolf, dog, or lion, fire, tree, or vulture, earth or water, or
what thou will'st, for thou art able so to do.'
Greek Magical Papyri

I

The business of unearthing, and establishing reference to, first causes belongs to the field of the psychologist, and, perhaps, the social anthropologist. The historian would claim no such concern, but he is affected, and his interest is engaged, in any attempt to trespass on, or abstract from, his own sphere.

Probably the most unexceptionable statement about the mind of 'early man' or 'proto-man' was made by Sir James Frazer. It is to be found in the closing pages of *The Golden Bough*. Early man's, and man's, approach to his life and environment is of two orders, religious and scientific, or magico-scientific. He did not use the term 'psychological', perhaps because he was not a biologist.

To a psychologist, there exists a body of psychological 'laws'. These contain references to instincts, reflexes, etc., and their conditioning under conditions of human development or evolution. This obscure field may itself stray across the boundaries of history, to the confounding of both. Thus psychologists have quite a circumstantial story to tell about the origins of human society and belief: and even Frazer himself was led to postulate certain essential human 'horrors', or inherent taboos.

II

The analysis of primitive society has constituted one of the

99

main preoccupations of thinkers of the 18th, 19th and 20th centuries A.D., and has been based fundamentally on observations of 'primitive' life made during those centuries. We will start by considering two of the most characteristic features of that society—totemism and exogamy.

Sir James Frazer begins his monumental work of that name with an early review of the subject in which he surmises that the institution of totemism was devised to enable members of a hunting and food-gathering culture to perform rites aimed at maintaining the supply of animals and plants: since these rites might be ineffective, however, if tribesmen were themselves, in the manner of the Walrus and the Carpenter, to kill and eat the immediate objects of the rites, totemic clans were subdivided into specific sections, each responsible for the promotion of one species, which it was itself forbidden to kill or eat.

Many savage tribes faithfully follow this ritual practice with its attendant taboos: many do not: the variant tribes are sometimes found in close contiguity, for instance in the York Peninsular of Northern Australia. Many tribes of South America are heretics. However, interest subsequently shifted to a new theory of origins. It was observed that savage women frequently connect the moment of quickening with the sight of some bird or animal, the propinquity of some striking natural feature, or the discovery in their clothing of an insect. This they take to be the creature or object that has 'impregnated' them.

So simple and obvious a solution of the problem presented by totemism—why a savage should believe himself to be related to, and descended from, a wild creature, plant, or inanimate object such as water—proved irresistable. The totem is in many cases a personal, and not a clan, possession, and this was deemed to be the primary type. It could be, and is, adopted on the prompting of a dream, signifying that the dreamer is under special protection. Why should

100

the individual totem became a clan totem? Probably, Frazer argued, because in the locality of the clan there was a natural feature that served as a harbour or breeding ground for a wild species—a rock that offered nesting facilities to wild pigeons, or a marsh haunted by the Olmec duck. This would be, surely, the proper venue for the formation of a Pigeon or Duck clan.

The exogamous/endogamous marriage system, sometimes referred to broadly, and not entirely accurately, as 'cross-cousin marriage', is frequently found in association with totemic institutions. This system involved the division of a tribe into two exogamous moieties, and in the majority of cases a further division into a number of classes. Sometimes the classes are themselves exogamous, and marriage is possible into another class of the same moiety. In its most complete and elaborate form, the system ensures that marriage is only possible across the moiety, and only between two specific classes: every class possesses its own exclusive complementary marriage class. Thus the choice for any marriage is restricted to half, a quarter, a sixth, an eighth, etc., of the entire tribe. Marriage into any unspecified class, even if the blood relationship were remote, constitutes a tabooed act, and is treated as incest. Husbands and wives are, of course, drawn from intermarrying classes: their children belong to the same class, either matrilineal or patrilineal, and cannot therefore intermarry.

Still concerned, in the manner of old-fashioned anthropology, with theories of origins, Sir James Frazer was of the view that this organisation was primarily designed to render impossible the marriage of parents and children, or of brothers and sisters, matters which, in sophisticated legal systems, require only the insertion of an appropriate clause. This complex manner of dealing with a simple prohibition was ascribed to a constitutional and inherent 'horror of incest'. It is, of course, perfectly permissible to marry a first cousin.

Sir James Frazer considered that the totemic system had only inadvertently become associated with an exogamous system. In fact, the two do not necessarily coincide, and it is frequently possible to marry into the personal totem, where the exogamous organisation permits.

III

The above is an over-simplification of its subject, but will suffice if we are to treat it, as was the intention, as an introduction to theories of origins. These have a separate and special importance, as they may lead us to issues that are fundamental to an understanding of the 'historical' development of the human outlook. Such a question should never be regarded as a mere topic for arm-chair speculation.

If we may attempt to extract some kind of a trend from the evidence as so far presented, it is broadly this:

(1) Totemism and exogamy are, in most existing instances, collective systems. As such, they are not necessarily favourable to 'individual' interpretations, such as dreams, theories of conception, innate horrors or self-taboos.

(2) If these systems were not developed in response to an innate human predeliction, they were probably developed through a need for a system. In other words, they could have served to satisfy their own object.

Let us give a possible example of the latter condition. A tribe, at a cultural hunting and food-gathering level, is in possession of a large tract of country, which it is required to exploit, and to protect from the incursions of other tribes. It is, of course, necessary to guard against the temptation to concentrate on easy areas, where food is normally plentiful. In conditions of early garden or hoe culture, this kind of idle slumming would be particularly undesirable. Thus it becomes expedient to divide the territory among a number of local sub-tribes, or clans, and maintain these clans at a proper establishment, and this expediency could lead to the construction of a full clan-exogamous system.

This territorial division, where it can be seen to exist, is in fact sometimes totemic, and sometimes exogamous. But, as Frazer pointed out, it should be considered quite proper, if you are a duck, to marry a duck, and not a fox.

A last word about taboos. Taboos are prohibitions, in savage thought, imposed by a divine ancestor—in other words, by an ancestor. Whatever the prohibition, any breach of it is likely to bring evil, or disastrous consequences. Sexual taboos have no pride of place in savage societies.

And a last word about totems. These involve a belief in a kinship with some object of the wild—animal, vegetable, mineral, or meteorological. They involve, perhaps incidentally, a concept of descent from the same object. But totemic ancestors are not generally regarded as Gods in the sense that the word is now understood.

IV

Kasyapa receives mention in the Hindu epics the Ramayana, the Mahabharata, and also in the Puranas. The Puranas are dated to the first few centuries of our era, the Ramayana to as early as 500 B.C., but all works contain collections of verbal lore, retained and transmitted in memory, and of incalculable age. Kasyapa is reputed to have been the grandfather of Manu, the first man and father of mankind. He was a tortoise, and the son of Time. He married thirteen of the daughters of Daksha, theologised as 'spiritual power'. These daughters became the progenitors of gods and demons, animals, birds, serpents, and certain heroes. One, for instance, Tamra, had six daughters: Suki, the mother of parrots, owls, and crows; Syeni, mother of hawks; Bhasi, mother of kites; Gridhrika, mother of vultures; Suchi, mother of water-fowl; Sugrivi, mother of horses, camels, and asses.

Another daughter of Daksha, named Krodhavasa, was the mother of cows and buffaloes; Ira the mother of trees, shrubs, and grass.

V

Totemism in Egypt was in decay in historical times: it was associated with the division of the country into what one is justified in calling tribes, because each claimed descent from a single ancestor. Each tribe possessed a banner which bore the emblem of an animal, bird, insect, weapon, natural feature and in one case the sun. This tribal organisation disappeared with the institution of kingship, though the office of chief may have been translated into a hereditary nobility. The 'sign' of the tribe was regarded as its deity and protector. Many of the animal signs were later numbered among the animal gods of Egypt, for example the hawk, the dog, the ibis, the lion, the bull.

Frankfort says (*Ancient Egyptian Religion*), 'The characteristic features of totemism, such as the claim of descent from the totem, its sacrifice for a ceremonial feast of the clan, and exogamy, cannot be found in Egyptian sources'. But we are tempted to quote the entire section from which this sentence is taken, for the light it throws on the way in which 'Early civilised man' thought of animals: 'SACRED ANIMALS AND OTHERNESS. There is one generic term which is most difficult to avoid when we discuss Egyptian religion. That is the word 'animal-gods'. It should not be used, as we shall show in a moment. But we must admit— and the Greek, Roman, and early Christian writers too were struck by the fact—that animals play an altogether unusual role in Egyptian religion. We cannot evade the issue by referring back to what we said a moment ago, namely, that the origin of cults is beyond our ken and that we shall never know how certain gods came to be associated with certain animals. There are too many gods showing such an association and their cult is too widespread for us to pretend to understand Egyptian religion without at least a tentative explanation of this its most baffling, most persistent, and to us most alien feature.

'It is wrong to say that the worship of animals is a survival from a primitive stratum of Egyptian religion. This view is often encountered and is supported by some plausible arguments. It is said that these cults are often of purely local significance; that they sometimes centre on quite insignificant creatures like the centipede or the toad; and that we must therefore place the sacred animals on a par with certain sacred objects, like the crossed arrows of the goddess Neith, and consider all these symbols as mere emblems of—and means of promoting—tribal unity. Some scholars have even interpreted them as totems. But the characteristic features of totemism, such as the claim of descent from the totem, its sacrifice for a ceremonial feast of the clan, and exogamy, can not be found in Egyptian sources. Moreover, any treatment of the sacred animals which stresses their local or political significance at the expense of their religious importance flies in the face of the evidence. It is undeniable that there is something altogether peculiar about the meaning which animals possessed for the Egyptians. Elsewhere, in Africa or North America, for example, it seems that either the terror of animal strength, or the strong bond, the mutual dependence of man and beast (in the case of cattle cults, for instance), explains animal worship. But in Egypt the animal as such, irrespective of its specific nature, seems to possess religious significance; and the significance was so great that even the mature speculation of later times rarely dispensed with animal forms in plastic or literary images referring to the gods.

'But there was nothing metaphorical in the connection between god and animal in Egypt. It is not as if certain divine qualities were made articulate by the creature, in the way the eagle elucidates the character of Zeus. We observe, on the contrary, a strange link between divinity and actual beast, so that in times of decadence animal worship may gain a horrible concreteness. Then one finds mummified cats, dogs, falcons, bulls, crocodiles, and so forth, buried by the hundreds in vast cemeteries which fill the Egyptologist with painful embarrassment—for this, we must admit, is polytheism with a vengeance. Nevertheless, these are grotesque but significant symptoms of a characteristic trait in Egyptian religion.

'To understand this trait, we should first realize that the relation between a god and his animal may vary greatly. If Horus is said to be a falcon whose eyes are sun and moon and whose breath is the cooling north wind, we may think that this was a mere image to describe an impressive god of the sky. But the god was depicted as a bird from the earliest times and was apparently believed to be manifest either in individual birds or in the species. Thoth was manifest in the moon, but also in the baboon and in the ibis and we do not know whether any relations were thought to exist between these different symbols, and if so, what they were. The relation between the Mnevis bull and the sun-god Re, and between the Apis bull and the earth-god Ptah, was different again. Ptah was never depicted as a bull or believed to be incarnate in a bull; but the Apis bull was called "The living Apis, the herald of Ptah, who carries the truth up-wards to him of the lovely face (Ptah)." The Mnevis bull bore a similar title in connection with Re. We have to deal here, moreover, not with a species considered sacred, but with one individual identified with certain marks, not as the incarnation, but as the divine servant of the god. Other deities were regularly imagined in animal shapes but even in their case the incarnation did not limit—it did not even define—their powers. Anubis, for instance, was most commonly shown as a reclining jackal but he was by no means a deified animal. Already in the earliest texts in which he is mentioned, he appears as the god of the desert cemeteries. He ensured proper burial and when mummification became common he counted as the master of embalmment. The god was depicted in papyri and reliefs with a human body and a jackal's head.

'Such hybrid forms are common in Egyptian art and the usual evolutionary theory explains them as 'transitional forms', intermediate between the 'crude' cult of animals and the anthropomorphic gods of a more enlightened age. This theory ignores the fact that the earliest divine statues which have been preserved represent the god Min in human shape. Conversely, we find to the very end of Egypt's independence that gods were believed to be manifest in animals. The goddess Hathor appears, for instance, in late papyri and even in royal statues as a cow. Yet she was rendered already in the First Dynasty, on the Palette of Narmer, with a human face, cow's horns, and cow's ears. This early appearance of human features was to be expected, for a god is personified power, and person-ification need not, but easily may, call up the human image. In any case, the gods were not confined to a single mode of manifestation. We have seen that Thoth appeared as moon, baboon, and ibis. He was also depicted as an ibis-headed man. To speak here of a transitional form seems pointless. There was no need for a transition. The god appeared as he desired, in one of his known manifestations. On the other hand, there was a definite need to distinguish deities when they were depicted in human shape, and in such an array the ibis-headed figure identified Thoth. I suspect that the Egyptians did not intend their hybrid designs as renderings of an imagined reality at all and that we should not take the animal-headed gods at their face value. These designs were probably pictograms, not portraits. Hathor, usually depicted as a cow, a woman's face with cow's ears, or as a woman wearing a crown of cow's horns (like Isis in the Frontispiece), appears very rarely as a cow-headed woman; the meaning would be: This is the goddess who is manifest in the cow. The animal-headed figures are quite unorganic and mechanical; it makes no difference whether a quadruped's head, an ibis' neck, or a snake's forepart emerge from the human shoulder. That again would be easily explained if they were only ideograms, and this interpretation is corroborated by the truly vital character of the few monsters invented by the Egyptians: Taurt, for instance, is convincing even though she is composed of incongruous parts: the head of a hippopotamus, the back and tail of a crocodile, the breasts of a woman, and the claws of a lion.

'Our rapid survey of the various relationships between gods and animals in Egypt does not clarify the role of the latter. But the very absence of a general rule and the variety of the creatures involved suggests, it seems to me, that what in these relationships became articulate was an underlying religious awe felt before all animal life; in other words, it would seem that animals as such possessed religious significance for the Egyptians. Their attitude might well have arisen from a religious interpretation of the animals' otherness. A recognition of otherness is implied in all specifically religious feeling, as Otto has shown. We assume, then, that the Egyptian interpreted the nonhuman as superhuman, in particular when he saw it in animals in their inarticulate wisdom, their certainty, their unhesitating achievement, and above all in their static reality. With animals the continual succession of generations brought no change; but this is not an abstract and far-fetched argument but something which suggested itself also to Keats for instance; in the "Ode to a Nightingale" he writes:

> Thou was not born for death, immortal Bird!
> No hungry generations tread thee down;
> The voice I hear this passing night was heard
> In ancient days by emperor and clown . . .

The animals never change, and in this respect especially they would appear to share—in a degree unknown to man—the fundamental nature of creation. We shall see in the following chapters that the Egyptians viewed their living universe as a rhythmic movement contained within an unchanging whole. Even their social order reflected this view; in fact, it determined their outlook to such an extent that it can only be understood as an intuitive—and therefore binding—interpretation of the world order. Now humanity would not appear to exist in this manner; in human beings individual characteristics outbalance generic resemblances. But the animals exist in their unchanging species, following their predestined modes of life, irrespective of the replacement of individuals. Thus animal life would appear superhuman to the Egyptian in that it shared directly, patently, in the static life of the universe. For that reason recognition of the animals' otherness would be, for the Egyptian, recognition of the divine.

'This interpretation of the animal cults of Egypt requires qualification in two respects; it depends, of course, on the strength which the vision of an unchanging universe can be proved to have possessed in Egypt, and it requires therefore the cumulative evidence of the subsequent chapters. And, furthermore, even if it is true that animals in general were capable of inspiring all Egyptians with a feeling of religious awe, that feeling assumed definite and different forms in each of the ensuing cults. Their variety is reflected in the relationships which were claimed to exist between gods and animals, whether individuals or whole species. The working out of such details falls outside the scope of this book. We shall merely say that some were worshipped in a very restricted area only, while others found recognition throughout the country.'

It is noteworthy that, in the third paragraph of our section, the author draws a comparison between classic Egyptian concepts and those of contemporary Africa and North America—a mere jump of 5000 years, but which reveals a fundamental difference or change of view-point.

Plutarch, in his study of the myths that deal with Isis and Osiris, refers briefly to traditions of a totemic organisation. He says that Osiris, when he set out on his campaign of world conquest (one of many features that establish his resemblance to Dionysus) divided his army into sections, to which he allotted ensigns bearing animal devices: these, he says, became objects of religious veneration to their followers. This, of course, is putting the cart before the horse, raising gods solely upon the edifice of their attribution or special circumstances, a view against which he specifically warns us:

'Transferring names of Gods to natures and to things that have no sense or soul, and which are necessarily destroyed by men according to their need and use.' (Plutarch, *Isis & Osiris,* sections LXVI & LXXII).

VI

For the major literary compilation of stories of the animal

metamorphoses of gods and humans we are indebted to Ovid. There are delightful echoes of these tales in the mythology of the aboriginal Australians.

The name Zeus is of Greek provenance, and derived from a root common to all Indo-European languages. Its application to the god traditionally associated with Crete undoubtedly masks an earlier Cretan appelation. The Cretan Zeus was born in a cave, and the circumstances of his birth reflect a large number of totemic associations. The infant Zeus was mysteriously separated from his mother, in the manner of other Hero traditions, and was suckled, or attended, variously, by a sow, a goat, bees, and doves. He was also associated with plants, for instance the willow, and he was possibly the consort of a willow goddess, who may in Crete have been Ariadne. Hesiod tells how he made the human race from ash-trees. He was worshipped orgiastically, in the manner of the Syrian mother goddesses, or of Dionysus, with whom his cult is to be compared.

One of his most interesting sacred marriages (to quote R. F. Willett in *Cretan Cults and Festivals,* surely the definitive authority on its subject in our period) 'was remembered at Hermione in the form of a totemic myth. Zeus often appears as a lover disguised as a bird, and it has been suggested that such myths, appearing in old Mycenean centres, recall the Minoan belief in the bird epiphanies characteristic of their goddess. In this case Zeus transformed himself into a cuckoo, on a mountain henceforth known as Cuckoo Mountain (Kokkygion)' (p. 51).

The birds whose terracotta images are found in domestic shrines recall the bird so often found iconographically perched on the double axe. This itself was regarded by Elliot Smith as a conventionalised eagle, an epiphany, with the bull, of the thunderer of Middle Eastern and Asiatic religions. His claws, for instance, are incorporated in the Tibetan thunder-dagger. All these birds are regarded by

Willett as epiphanies (p. 73), but we are here concerned with an aspect of the totemic complex which singles out certain creatures and plants for their special symbolic significance, or ritual usefulness. Such, for instance, was surely the vulture, whose shrine has been unearthed at Catal Huyuk, the Neolithic town in Anatolia whose fluorit carries us back many thousands of years before the palace period of Crete. The vulture, here as in Egypt probably associated with a goddess, may have officiated in a mortuary cult, with the function of consuming the flesh of the dead.

The sacred marriages of the gods also carry us back to the age of goddesses, or rather of the Great Goddess, and the totemic animals that reared the infant Zeus were undoubtedly themselves epiphanies of this primordial figure.

The following passage from Mr Willett's book (p. 78) illustrates certain associations of the Goddess: 'It is clear, from certain of the monuments, from the nomenclature of later deities, and from mythology, that the goddess was a moon-goddess as well as (or rather by virtue of being) a fertility-goddess. The worship of the moon in its various phases is closely associated with the time-keeping which is indispensable to any moderately advanced agricultural community. This aspect of the subject must be discussed when the problem of the calendar is considered. But moon-worship must also have contributed to the cult of the goddess from the point of view of human fertility and from the special associations of the moon with the physiological functions of women. Sacrificial animals offered by women to the moon universally belong to small species, chiefly the hare, goat and pig; the dove, especially in Semitic women's cults; and the cat. The close relationship of the Cretan goddess with the goat and the dove needs no emphasis, and the pig and the cat are represented in a variety of contexts. The general choice of these small species was probably associated with the domestication of animals, the huntsmen bringing home the young which the women kept as pets. The snake, as a fertility symbol accompanying the goddess as protectress of the household, is likely to have been under the special provenance of women in a similar way, except that it was not sacrificed.

'The moon is commonly regarded, in primitive societies, as the stimulus of fertility in plants and vegetation. The tending of plants was included among the early social tasks of women, and herbal magic is everywhere their province, since plants, flowers and seeds were commonly used by women at menstruation, child-birth and pregnancy. The lily was, above all, the Minoan sacred flower. Ritual dances take place before the goddess in a field of lilies; a lily appears at her feet when she is enthroned; she is offered a bunch of lilies by her female attendants. Sometimes she is offered poppy capsules. As late as the time of Pliny, the lily was considered to be a check to menstruation; and the poppy for long continued to be regarded as a symbol of fecundity.'

VII

In savage societies, and where totems are held individually, an individual may indicate the vehicle of his next incarnation. It may be an animal or a plant, but to his descendants it becomes taboo as food. This is evidently the Orphic or Brahminical or Jain prohibition, but with a bias in favour of close kindred.

It is common to believe in reincarnation within the tribe, or within a locality, which latter belief impels some savages to bury deceased children at the roadside. Burial in houses was a feature of early neolithic times, and when the practice was falling into disuse in early Crete it was maintained in the case of children. Ancestral names were regularly revived for the newly-born. Some of these were associated with the totem, or were actually the word for a part of the totem.

The process of reincarnation is frequently controlled by a tribal ancestor, culture hero, or ghostly woman or (Red Indian) Old Woman in the Sky.

The Urabunna of Australia held that every individual is the reincarnation of a spirit that has emanated from the body of an ancestor of the Dream-time. This ancestor was half animal or half plant, in fact a totemic entity.

The evidence is sufficiently extensive to justify the conclusion that a tribe or clan is perpetuated by reincarnation.

In the appalling confusion of savage concepts and beliefs we are left once again with the impression of a system once clear and logical that has become faint and blurred, the effect of retaining across great stretches of time a philosophy that was never fully understood, and that was allowed to linger on when more alert communities had changed to something better.

W. J. Perry goes so far as to say, in *The Children of the Sun,* 'It does not seem that the semi-human, semi-animal ancestor of the clan plays any part, or that a notion of a totem is essential for the constitution of the clan. Rather would it seem that the totemic clan is an artificial construction, and not an organic institution with interdependent parts. The perpetuation of the clan evidently depends solely on the idea of the reincarnation, through the women, of the spirit individuals.'

This is a reasonable conclusion to arrive at, yet a curious one, in a world of such extensive and variegated animal and plant associations. W. J. Perry was, of course, building up an argument to support the premises of the special diffusionist school of Elliot Smith, and shortly makes the claim that the dim tribal culture heroes of America and Oceania were, in fact, missionaries and speculators from Egypt. This specific suggestion is a chronological and circumstantial monstrosity, yet in its path of error and over-emphasis the school can be credited with many interesting observations and summaries.

How different is the observation made by Mr R. F. Willetts in the classic work from which we have already quoted. He is drawing a comparison between what he believes to be the totemic concepts of Paleolithic Man in Europe and Western Asia, and those still traceable in the local traditions and the myths of ancient Crete—a hypothetical culture sequence that would once have been regarded as partaking of the fabulous, yet now that the rear frontiers of the Neolithic age have been pushed so far back, in both Anatolia and Eastern Europe, and vestiges of the Palaeolithic age are so close to them in time and place, can, with reservations, be granted an introductory paragraph in human, and Western, pre-history.

'The life and death of animals and human beings are indissolubly linked, and the relationship becomes objectified in the form of totemic representations, symbolic alike of ancestry and rebirth'.

In other words, in the view of the palaeolithic hunter, man and the animal were linked throughout a sequence of lives. We have already suggested that the habit of Magdalenian man of committing his animal paintings to the walls and ceilings of caves hardest of access must have had an object, and that this object was to protect his totem from defacement by natural or enemy action, and at the same time place it as close as possible to the inaccessible innermost recesses of the cave, the province of the Mother Goddess and perhaps of the ancestors. In effect it also served as an early form of the well-known 'external soul', which guaranteed the hunter's reincarnation in the totemic animal.

These speculations we hope will be taken by the reader

on trust, as a lead in the direction of a solution of the problem of 'origins' rather than as an Aunt Sally.

A further quotation from Mr Willetts will carry the argument a stage forward: 'The migration of the Gravettians from Lake Baikal to the Atlantic seaboard is marked by the "Venus" figurines which tend to be replaced at later stations (notably la Ferrassie in the Vesere valley, where the whole development is documented) by more or less conventional symbols of the vagina or by pregnant animals. Most telling among these allusions is, however, the siting of the sanctuaries in caves. What a "kloof enclosed with hills and precipices" was to the bushmen, the cave was to the northern hunters: the magic womb in which the fertility of the totem was maintained. To these sacred rites only the initiated could penetrate. To enter the Montespan cave, for example, one must dive beneath an overhanging rock through an ice-cold stream . . . Nor are we left in any doubt, in the light of the evidence quoted, concerning the rituals of creation which took place in these sacred enclosures. They are also, moreover, vividly illustrated in post-glacial settings by paintings or engravings in which a man and a woman are linked by a line which is then carried around them, like a cave or stone-circle.'

At the present time, belief in reincarnation is held widely throughout Asia, being an essential article in both the Buddhist and the Hindu faiths. These beliefs take us back to the beginnings of literacy, that is to say in Asia prior to our era. The Karma of the Hindus is associated with the Gods, in the system of Buddhism it is not, but this was an offshoot of Hinduism. Animal reincarnation is treated as a punishment, or as in the case of the Buddha himself, an act of voluntary sacrifice.

Classic Egyptian religious systems dispensed with the phenomenon of metempsychosis, as the wider fate of kings or king-gods drew the multitude after it. Nevertheless, the literature of ancient Egypt does indeed contain stories of episodes involving reincarnation, in which, for instance, personal hostilities are carried over from one incarnation to another.

The belief survived in Egypt into the times of Plutarch, who in the treatise to which we referred above, stigmatises the faith in a rebirth of humans into animal forms as 'incredible' (LXII). Evidently this was an ancient cult, one of many that persisted among the people underneath the facades of orthodoxy, and may have influenced the Orphic cult in Greece.

In the course of the slow diffusion and decline of ideas, we have seen the Venus of the caves grow into the Mother Goddess and Moon Goddess of the Middle East, and degenerate into the Old Woman in the Sky. Everywhere in our historical references we have seen totemic animals as vehicles of divinity. Among savages of our era, on the other hand, the gods and goddesses have become remote— the 'deus otiosus' of Mr. Mircea Eliade—or cruel, eccentric, fearful, and the controller of the totem is the shadow of an ancestor.

VIII

The historian is one who looks for major landmarks and main directions. The anthropologist seeks out the principles of belief and practice, in their current setting, and must take serious notice of exceptions and diversions, since any of these may prove to possess some significance, provide a clue to the working of the savage mind, or reveal its reaction to special circumstances. The latest worker of distinction in the field of anthropology, and particularly of the study of savage societies, is M. Levi-Strauss, who brings to the task a mind of exceptional clarity and analytical power.

To one admiring dissenter his approach seems to display one occupational failing, in that he credits the objects of his studies with a like power of analysis, albeit employed, contrary to orthodox views on the evolution of thought, without complementary benefit of language. What would his models have said, had they been able to speak academic French? Or what would M. Levi-Strauss' thesis have sounded like in the Arunta dialect? Nevertheless, his analysis of the operations of contemporary totemism and exogamy is new and exciting, and as valid as such a study will ever be. It is not, however, rounded into a system, and consequently seems overladen with useless and perverse activity, and frustrating prohibitions. In *The Savage Mind*, M. Levi-Strauss confesses that the full task would, in all probability, prove impossible of accomplishment without the use of a computer.

We will turn, therefore, and in conclusion of this brief essay, from an anthropologist to a historian, a psychological historian, who has exercised vast influence in a small and distressed field.

It is evidently a well-established habit of the human mind to receive any system, viewed externally and objectively, as a closed one. The paranoiac thinks that society has mustered its ranks against him. The social climber sees himself as standing out in a drawing-room like a scarecrow in a field of spring wheat. The psychologist gropes round in the purlieus of animal and sub-human life for a key to the behaviour of the same drawing-room.

The ardent grecophil of sixteenth century Europe envisaged the Gods of Olympus as eternal and unchanging as Gods ought to be. And the anthropologist of this century treats his subject matter as a key which, correctly turned, will expose to his view the habits of thought of 'primitive or early' man.

It is true that M. Levi-Strauss is aware of changes that

have taken place in his material at some time or other. Hence his characteristic lack of dogmatism and dislike of fixed terms. He has rejected the term 'totemism' as we have, ideally, rejected the word 'fertility'. It is absurd to dismiss the tribal urge for continuity as analogous to the farmer's concern for his crops. Nevertheless, M. Levi-Strauss' untiring and luminous work is incomplete without the services of a historian.

The Greek gods were continuously changing, and the historian is aware of this state of flux, and of the all-embracing flux of history, of the history of human affairs and of the study of history itself. At the same time he is searching for an absolute, because this is apparently an innate need of the human mind.

A scholar of the calibre of M. Levi-Strauss would never regard the world of his interests as a closed one. Not so the psycho-analyst, or the worshippers at the shrine of Jung, the latterday hero-worshipper. Their world has not changed for some tens of thousands of years: its beginning is masked in assumption without evidence: and because science, unlike scholarship, does not demand evidence, that beginning is with us still.

Freud put forward the hypothesis that early homo sapiens lived in herds on the pattern of many wild species, where one male is dominant and drives out the younger males as they become adults. One day the young of the herd banded together, killed the dominant male, and took over the women. This act resulted in over-powering feelings of guilt, which prompted the males to exalt the memory or spirit of the dead father into a totem, which they respected throughout the year, but ate ceremonially on one day of the year in celebration—or to express it more explicitly—in renewal of the act of liberation. Exogamous taboos were subsequently established to keep peace within the tribe.

It should not be necessary to treat this theorem as one

to be contended with, since there is no evidence which might serve as grounds for contention. One can, however, raise certain valid objections, by presenting simple alternatives that are open to demonstration. Guilt feelings are, in the main, a feature of religions that originated in Babylonia, and probably reflected the precarious conditions of life in that area. There also, and elsewhere, they seem to originate in fear of the jealousy of the dead generally, that is to say of the immediately dead, and thus the living are careful not to boast of their blessings, count their people or flocks, or display their wealth ostentatiously—the 'sin' of hubris. They become 'guilty' about their advantages, and acquire merit with acts of generosity to the poor.

The totem is not respected in the shape of a human, male or female, and can be associated with a Mother Goddess, or so the evidence strongly suggests. The ceremonial eating of the totem is an early act of communion, and nowhere suggests liberation. No guilt feelings have been remarked in the savage's attitude to his totem. Only the practical reason given for the custom of exogamy—the need to avoid internecine strife—could be valid, but not if a male were granted prior right in the possession of a sister, or the nearest available kin.

Let us now turn to another argument of Freud's. *Beyond the Pleasure Principle* deals with questions of pain and death, their cultivation and pursuit. Freud propounded the theory of the Death Wish, which he exalted into a primary constituent of the human psyche. It is allied, in his view, with the phenomenon of masochism, and sadism is described as a projection of masochism on to another person. In an extraordinary section of the above-quoted work, he asks what is the true object of the migratory habits of wild species. What is the purpose of this weary shuttling to and fro? Of course, he answers, it is an expression of an innate weariness of life, an ever-recurring restlessness, a desire for release and death.

It is easy to assert the contrary, that men, savages, and wild creatures will fight desperately for life. But there is a positive and simpler alternative. The 'fetishes', the elements of sexual selection, serve also in the process of tumescence, of sex play. Sadism and masochism are expressions of the psychic difference between the sexes, and can also serve as fetishes. Their use in sex play is obvious, and was examined exhaustively by Havelock Ellis. Animals will fight for a mate, but do not exercise sexual violence. If this argument is invalid in our context, Ockham's knife has become mysteriously blunt.

Magdalenian man has left behind him prolific traces of the terrible and long prolonged fight he waged for existence. What were his motives? First, the instinct for survival, individually and collectively. Second, the pleasure he found in life, and his pursuit of that pleasure. He was the greatest meat-eater in human history. We assume that he loved hunting, and certain of his descendants spoke of the 'happy hunting grounds'. His pictures suggest that he appreciated nature aesthetically, and that he enjoyed his religion. If circumstances compelled him to live in the mouths of caves, he would nevertheless possibly be described as the first civilised man. Our cities are still little more than elaborated caves.

He is an example to us all, and I should like to have met him. Sometimes I fancy I have.

IX

Some apology would be called for for essaying a work of detection such as this in the wake of Miss G. R. Levy's *The Gate of Horn*, were it not that the writer wishes to draw attention to vital matters of emphasis.

Miss Levy's work is surely a classic answer to the writer's plea that what has been hitherto loosely included in the sphere of 'anthropology' should be treated historically. As reference to her book can show, a historic approach is the only possible means of dispersing the appalling miasma of vagueness and conflict that is exhaled in the course of a purely one-dimensional study. Miss Levy gives much thought to the intimate connection between the Mother Goddess of Palaeolithic times and the essentially cave complexion of their cults. We would only reinforce, with the assistance of other authorities, the fundamentally theistic nature of what came to be identified as—or termed—totemism, the strength of the quest for reincarnation, usually in its origins animal reincarnation, and the theistic basis proper to a belief in reincarnation.

The half-man, half-animal figures of Mediterranean mythology have never been more than half explained. Fifty years ago it was said—by whom we cannot now swear, though it was certainly one of the reigning authorities in early Greek studies, or one of the dominant school of anthropologists—possibly Gilbert Murray or Frazer—that the Pan type of spirit was 'evidence of evolution from a previous animal cult.' This was an 'easy' explanation which, at that rudimentary stage of Palaeolithic researches, took no cognisance of the animal travesties of cave paintings, wherein animal and man were already fused.

Reincarnation is probably still the most powerful idea in world religion: yet it has (as the revivalist would put it) lost God, or the concept of the godhead which came into the life of early man out of the bowels and substance of earth. Is it any wonder that the itinerant anthropologist sees so little force in the contemporary savage's ideas regarding that remote and ineffectual spirit? Or that Eastern Mediterranean religion declined into state and fertility practices, leaving the multitudes to witchcraft and superstition?

The history of culture is one of change and decay, due primarily to a diminution of individual participation. The needs of masses can be assessed statistically, and lend themselves to material systems of observance: there is a decline into cynicism and pessimism: is not a man's soul even now, and more than ever, in our faiths of Works, weighed against a loaf of bread?

The Australian Churinga, or individual incarnation fetish, is matched with similar cryptically marked fetishes found in Palaeolithic caves.

It can be accepted that primitive man lived and operated in groups. There is no evidence that he was organised into tribes.

There is no evidence that primitive man engaged in Ancestor Worship, or brought ancestors into his cult practices.

Reincarnation, evidenced for instance by the recurrence of individual names, is universally manipulated as an individual phenomenon.

How did the concept, so rich in iconography and tradition, of Lady of the Animals or Lord of the Animals, with whom the Shaman holds converse, come into being?

Could primitive man have regarded reincarnation, into animal or man, as a Law of Nature?

Would he understand what we mean by a Law of Nature?

DARK FRONTIER

The Nats do not like the smell of soap.
Village Headman to Civil Officer, Wa States,
1937, in the Author's presence

Stupid river, dull wood, obtuse field.
Taoist response to cleverness, (*circa* 500 B.C.)

We cannot think of a time that is oceanless.
T. S. Eliot, *Four Quartets*

I

Between the two Wars, a school of anthropology flourished which denied historicity, and attributed all savage myths, rituals, and practices to the immediate needs of the community. Even a myth was held to be the expression, in story form, of some necessary taboo. This concept was closely related to the doctrine of dialectical materialism. It was held, quite rightly, that it was the business of the Colonial —or Trust—Administrator to study the habits and ways of thought of his charges, in order that he should assist them to live in accordance with their own traditions and ingrained habits. Any attempt to impose alien customs and ways of thought were—again surely quite rightly—deprecated. The injuries inflicted by international commerce and missionary activity were all too well understood, and by then quite irreparable.

Dialectical materialism is a sound principle of history, but a bad law. Societies and individuals are subject to incessant change, and the diffusion of ideas, habits, and technical processes is a common agent of this change, though not the only one.

In *The Adventures of the Black Girl in her Search for God,* Bernard Shaw refers disparagingly to 'The Caravan of the Curious'. These are the intelligentsia who are interested in primitive peoples from other motives than their immediate welfare and betterment. Yet he should have considered, being himself in part a Celt, that emergent peoples are themselves the keenest students of their origins, and if

127

not provided with an authentic history, will inevitably create one.

Throughout the world there are certain common denominators of idea and practice. The variety and variation of emphasis to be found is so enormous that a logical summary, even in one specific area such as Oceania, would be impossible, as M. Levi-Strauss has said, without the services of a computer. In fact the pure anthropologist is better advised to stick to the study of one area, with all its corruptions of original, and lost, ideas, since other areas will only provide him with other corruptions.

A study of diffusion is concerned with real history, with the movement of peoples and ideas, and with the rise and decline of those ideas. It interests itself in the origin of cultures, their adoption, transformation, and loss. It constitutes, indeed, an appeal to Curiosity, an interest in, and love of, the world. Because history without curiosity is like religion without imagination, a stunted and utilitarian handbook to contemporary affairs, a day-to-day guide for economists and ethical jurists.

II

A treatment of the theme of Cultural Diffusion in relation to Europe and Asia would soon grow to the magnitude of a universal history. As applied to Polynesia, the question becomes merged with that of origins, since the culture and the people are homogenous, and arrived in comparatively recent times. The expansion of the Bantu peoples of Equatorial and South Africa is likewise of very recent date, and there is an imponderable factor in the influence exercised, with or without volition, by Egypt of pre-dynastic and dynastic times. Of the early history of the Americas we know little: such written records as exist are of late date, the area is enormous, and the background of conformation, climate, and natural life is extremely varied.

Thus we propose to take as the text for this essay two special cases, which reflect, positively or negatively, on each other.

The civilisation of Peru, which may be dated in origin to the beginning of the first millenium B.C., possessed the craft of metallurgy, but not that of writing. The civilisation of the Olmecs is recorded from much the same period of emergence. The Olmecs employed hieroglyphs in inscript-ions: their later successors, the Mayas, made no use of metals before the end of the first millenium A.D.

Neither culture possessed the wheel or the plough, nor did either employ animals for draught, with the possible exception, at an unknown date, of the llama of the Andes. Stock breeding was not practised. Both cultures worked in stone, producing magnificent sculpture and cyclopean architecture: the Peruvians dispensed with any kind of mortar, their masonry being cut and fitted with extraordin-ary precision.

It is not the object of this essay to venture more fully into the problems of specific influences: Elliot Smith and his school made a case, and produced much evidence, for including the Americas in a wider—in fact a world—cultural complex, which they termed the 'Archaic Civil-isation'. Thor Heyerdahl's monumental work *American Indians in the Pacific* is a definitive treatment of the quest-ion; it was published in 1952, and has not to our know-ledge received a definitive answer. The debate is still open: all that need be said for our purpose is that there is much variation in matters of detail and method, but little differ-ence in principle, between the civilisation of the Americas at their flower, and those of the Old World, if we regard as matters of principle the existence of organised states, kings, priests, and hierarchies, gods human and animal, cosmic, natural, and functional, temples, arts and crafts, war and armies.

III

The curious and basic shortcomings of the two civilisations to which we have alluded suggest in some respects a gap in mutual communication, and in others a lack of the slightest suspicion of the presence of another world beyond the seas. However, neither of these deductions may fit the circumstances at all.

In the first place, we have to consider what we may term the ritual conservatism of all people, ancient and modern, primitive or sophisticated, whose daily lives are governed by religion. We may take as an example the superstitious awe with which primitive people regarded and handled iron. Although we have no records of the period, bronze and other metals probably aroused identical feelings in the days of their early development. It is conceivable that sheer necessity alone provided justification for the earliest practical employment of metals, in fact that they were first employed in war, for the protection of the shrines of the gods. Thus there is an early Egyptian legend which deals with the coming of the people of the Winged Disk, the earliest recorded bearers of metal weapons. Certainly, well into historic times stone was used in substitution of metal for ritual purposes. Flint knives were employed, for instance, in ancient Israel for the ceremony of circumcision, and in Egypt for embalming the bodies of the dead. The extraction and smelting of metal from the substance of Mother Earth, in itself an impious outrage, was probably legitimised in the Old World by, for instance, the marriage of Hephaestus and Aphrodite, or Vulcan and Venus. However, the metal itself later became sacred,

130

perhaps through its 'response' to fire, and the sacred double axe of Crete may have served to equate the metal, through analogy with the eagle, with the divinity of the sun.

War was a feature of tribal or national life in the Americas from Neolithic times, and was waged with weapons of stone, wood, bone, etc. But the scale of battle could never have approached that of Europe and Asia where geographical conditions permitted the growth of huge and closely knit empires, and unimpeded movement across vast areas; and the civilisation of Peru and Central America could never, at any time in their history, have come into conflict.

In China of the Shang-Yin Dynasty, where the art of bronze casting appeared in a state of full maturity, the material was first used exclusively for weapons and other war material (horse harness and so on), and for ritual vessels, including drums. These uses would not strike us as constructive or economic (in the categorical sense).

IV

The plough was developed in Europe for the cultivation on a large scale of the type of product which demanded it—in fact of cereals, both wet and dry. The gradual spread of neolithic farming communities across Europe involved also a time-lag in the evolution of agricultural methods, even those well known and practised in the Middle East, and the heavy plough, for instance, was only introduced into England in Anglo-Saxon times.

Everywhere in the world, a garden economy preceded that of heavy agriculture, and even in the ancient Middle East persisted well into historic times in the areas best suited to it, such as the islands of the Mediterranean. Echoes of this phase of history, and of its religious associations, linger on in the names of the classical gods and goddesses of gardens and orchards, flower and fruit. Cultivation on this scale remained the prerogative of women, as the recognised agents of fertility, and to this day the planting of rice in South-East Asia is largely delegated to women.

The staple food crop of the Americas is maize, which was probably evolved in Mexico, and reached Peru before the classical period. This crop, like rice, is planted individually. The rows of maize can be interspersed with the other staple food plants, gourds, pumpkins, squashes, and various kinds of bean. Potatoes became a major food product, and in tropical areas the manioc and yam were developed.

All these plants require a garden rather than a field type of production and care, and with it, the use of a hoe or digging stick rather than of a plough.

A plough demands the services of a draught animal of some kind, and the question here arises—why did the peoples of the Americas take no trouble to domesticate animals, with the exception of poultry, and the virtually ubiquitous dog? Well, in the first place, it is a matter of some doubt whether this question concerns the phenomenon of diffusion at all. It is evident in the fact that, for instance, the turkey and some species of duck were domesticated, that the *idea* of domestication was well understood in the Americas. Wild life, however, somewhat overshadowed human life, and in the ages of which we are treating hunting was a prolific source of food, and yet never so easy that it could lead to the decimation of the natural quarry. It is interesting to wonder what would have been the course of human history in Central Asia had the horse never existed. Perhaps life on the steppes would have been much like life on the prairies of North America before the coming of the horse led to the extinction of the vast herds of buffalo and bison. Hunting and fishing people possess a god-given way of life, and cling to it until they are driven out of it by a failure of material, or by a sharp rise in their own numbers.

V

That the *idea* of the wheel was familiar to the people of the Americas is clear from the fact that they made wheeled toys.

The earliest evidence for the existence of the wheel is derived from Mesopotamian reliefs of about 3000 B.C. It was made of wood, not, as is commonly supposed, a transverse cut across a tree-trunk, but a simple construction of planks. We may assume that it was made with stone tools, since bronze was not in general use at this time.

We can offer here a close analogy with the craft of ship-making in the Americas, though at a very much later date. The sea-going canoes of the Indians of N.W. America— roughly what is now British Columbia—were hollowed out of trees, and built up with cut planks, the whole process being effected with stone implements. Thus, even these 'primitive' peoples possessed the technical competence to construct a wheel: although it must be borne in mind that the process of shipbuilding may have been acquired from the fishermen of N.E. Asia, and we are dealing with a date about the beginning of our era. Why, although they possessed both the idea of the wheel, and the necessary materials, did none of the American peoples take the modest step of constructing this foundation of human industry and progress?

No plea on utilitarian grounds can be accepted: that communities were small, and distances not great: that the terrain was better suited to human porterage: that slaves were plentiful (but this would have applied only to the

133

emergent nations): that there were no draught animals (but would not a hand cart have been welcome?).

There is certainly an economic argument of some validity. Wheel-making is an industry, and primitive hunting or gardening communities cannot afford industries. These become supportable only when there exist cities or states that can maintain specialist craftsmen, and by this time the rulers may be content with the muscles of their subjects' backs. It is safe to say that our first records of the wheel in the Old World are coeval with the early dynasties in Mesopotamia, when the Sumerians, certainly not less than the most brilliant race in history, were approaching their cultural peak. A wheel could conceivably at one time have stood in for the carriage of aristocratic Europe. In the writer's young days, the term 'carriage folk' was still in common use.

The argument is an inconclusive one. There is, however, another which may be more relevant to our subject. The Sumerians, as far as the evidence goes, not only built the first wheel, but were the first men to conceive of the possibilities of the wheel. But even if they themselves took the idea, or prototype, from an earlier people, a significant point still remains to be made: the possibility of the wheel was not a *natural* one. Houses are natural, many creatures construct shelters or elaborate caves: ships are natural, witness the Nautilus: a single disc is natural, and the sun was sometimes depicted in this form: but wheels that rotate on an axle not only do not exist in nature, but they could not exist. To make use of a piece of current jargon, they broke every rule.

Let us be patient, and pause before we condemn this plea as an irrelevant caprice. We are speaking of ways of thought that are totally alien to our own, and to illustrate it we would quote a passage from Arthur Waley's *Three Ways of Thought in Ancient China,* from the section devoted to the writings of the Taoist Chuang Tsu:

The Taoists objected to machinery. There are of course many grounds upon which labour-saving devices may be condemned. The common modern objection is that they cause unemployment: but religious leaders (Gandhi, for example) reject them on the ground that they have a degrading effect on those who use them. The Taoist objection was of the latter kind: 'Tzu-kung, the disciple of Confucius, after travelling to Ch'u in the south, came back by way of Chin. When he was passing through Han-yin he saw an old man who was engaged in irrigating his vegetable plots. The way this old man did it was to let himself down into the well-pit by footholes cut in the side and emerge clasping a pitcher which he carefully emptied into a channel, thus expending a great deal of energy with very small results. "There exists", Tzu-kung said to him, "a contrivance with which one can irrigate a hundred vegetable plots in a single day. Unlike what you are doing, it demands a very small expenditure of energy, but produces very great results. Would you not like me to tell you about it?" The gardener raised his head and gazed at Tzu-kung. "What is it like?", he asked. "It is an instrument carved out of wood", said Tzu-kung, "heavy behind and light in front. It scoops up the water like a bale, as quickly as one drains a bath-tub. Its name is the well-sweep". A look of indignation came into the gardener's face. He laughed scornfully, saying, "I used to be told by my teacher that where there are cunning contrivances there will be cunning performances, and where there are cunning performances there will be cunning hearts. He in whose breast a cunning heart lies has blurred the pristine purity of his nature; he who has blurred the pristine purity of his nature has troubled the quiet of his soul, and with one who has

135

troubled the quiet of his soul Tao will not dwell. It is not that I do not know about this invention; but that I should be ashamed to use it.

We must then "bind the fingers" of the technicians, "smash their arcs and plumb-lines, throw away their compasses and squares." Only then will men learn to rely on their inborn skill, on the "Great Skill that looks like clumsiness." But the culture-heroes were not the only inventors who "tampered with men's hearts." Equally pernicious (as will be seen in the next section) were on the one hand the Sages, inventors of goodness and duty, and of the laws which enforce an artificial morality; and on the other, the Tyrants, inventors of tortures and inquisitions, "embitterers of man's nature."

VI

The economic and ritualistic aspects of our subject stand in an uneasy relationship to each other, a marriage of historical necessity, meaning by this phrase what actually happened, not what might have happened, ought to have happened, or was bound to happen. Historical necessity in the latter sense is the abracadabra of the charlatan or the ignoramus. The picture we can dimly perceive unfolding before us in the early Americas is one of a contumacious priesthood establishing itself over a poor and lowly troop of villagers or tribesmen. But let us call for better lighting of this stage. Priests and huntsmen are commonly united in an inflexible conservatism, and if the peasant wishes for anything more, it is for more land.

Since a written script developed in only one small area of this vast continent, it may be timely here to epitomise what we think we know of the development of scripts in the old world.

The majority of scripts appear to have been devised for

strictly practical purposes, and this is why their interpretation has so frequently been attended by disappointment rather than elation. The Egyptian and Sumerian texts that constitute their literature are fully developed. The early texts of peoples who have followed them in acquiring the art of writing seem mainly to have been used for purposes of commerce and records. The 'literary' texts were produced by fully fledged states of ancient provenance. Others have presented greater difficulty because, by their very nature, they are fragmentary.*

Although Egyptian hieroglyphic texts, for instance, were the property of the priesthood, other priesthoods have in practice demonstrated their disdain for the written word and, partly for obscurantist reasons, have relied on the transmission of their 'secrets' by word of mouth and memory, as witness the ante-literate material of the Indo-European, Persian, and Celtic hierarchies.

Thus it may be taken as matter for congratulation when a script is developed, rather than as surprise when it is not. It does appear to indicate a high development of industry and trade, and the existence of what one is justified in describing as an entrepreneur class, an early bourgeoisie, possessing some degree of independence in the exercise of its ambitions.

Taking into account what we have postulated in this essay, there is a prima facie case for supposing that the civilisation of Peru arose out of the fairly sudden imposition of a priestly aristocracy on a primitive and unorganised tribal community. The lack of the wheel and of a written language both point to this conclusion, and the same principle might, with reservations, apply to the Olmec civilisation of the Tabasco area on the gulf of Mexico, where hieroglyphic inscriptions occur, and a toy wheeled cart has been

*In fact, I and II dynastic Egyptian script consists mainly of labels, jar sealings, and inscriptions on stone and pottery vessels.

unearthed.

VII

Stone provided man with many of his earliest tools, and he could handle it with familiarity. Its uses included, inter alia, the shaping of stone. Its architectural properties lend themselves to the satisfaction of man's only enduring passion, that for immortality or return. The Australian Churinga, which may possess a prototype in European palaeolithic sites, is an individually marked stone which seems to be linked with the soul.

Stone circles, usually associated with ritual pits, which seem designed to give access from the underworld,may be intended to provide earthly vestment for the ancestral spirits, when they are called to attend the tribal or state council. The portrait statue in Egyptian Mastaba tomb chapels certainly served this purpose. In Egypt, the stone sarcophagus was used to safeguard the dead body, which nevertheless then had to be embalmed, as stone does not serve as a preservative, except for the soul.

Building in stone demands so high a standard of sculptural and architectural technique, and entails the use of manpower on so vast a scale, that only a wealthy and highly centralised state could undertake it on any significant scale. Stone architecture was a late importation into Central and Eastern Asia, being introduced by way of Persia. Although it may be held with some conviction that the people of India were the greatest architects and sculptors in the history of the world, they did not develop their stone temple architecture until after the time of Alexander, and the 'idea' was probably derived from the Persian and Greek example, notwithstanding that their designs owed little or nothing to these sources.

138

The stone erections of Micronesia and Polynesia could only, culturally speaking, have been interpolations from outside sources, and the labour force is likely to have been imported also, since the manpower employed on the immense port construction at Ponape, for instance, must have exceeded far the resources of the Caroline islands.

The present Polynesians arrived in their habitat in the first millenium of our era, and were, as surface archaeology has suggested, the first truly domiciled occupants. Tradition in most of the islands relates that these cyclopean works were in situ when they arrived. Thus their precise date is still a matter of doubt. The question is alluded to here, since the time factor would suggest that the builders, or the stimulus to building, were unlikely to have come from Asia, or anywhere else in the West.

The stone temples and palaces of Peru have been assigned a date towards the end of the first millenium B.C., while Central American architecture developed over a long period from its beginnings with the Olmecs early in the first millenium B.C. The vast stone heads that characterise this very idiosyncratic people were among their earliest works: they have been compared with similar heads found in Tihuanaco and Sumatra, and the same singular and expressive style adorns the temples of Ankor-Vat, whose date may be a thousand years later.

It should be evident that to draw up a world-wide lineage of masonry, in terms either of chronology or style, would, in our present state of knowledge, be quite impossible. Architecture reveals, as fully as does any of the fine arts, the character of its creator. Certain patterns are, indeed, basic, particularly the pyramid and the pylon, which from Silbury Hill to Palenque, constitute a kind of primeval Welt-Kunst. In its flower, it becomes the signature of a race, fallen though it may be in some respects from the simplicity or grandeur of its beginnings.

These beginnings lie in a certain religious attitude which we have suggested is of a particular kind, and the availability of a centralised pool of wealth and labour, under centralised and absolutist control. Special conditions are required for the development of a stone architecture, and the idea itself may not be of spontaneous conception, since it is altogether non-utilitarian and remote from practical common sense. A cyclopean monument discovered in a remote jungle captivates us by its improbability. To echo the Magic Flute, only the gods could inhabit such a place. And the gods are great travellers.

VIII

This closing essay of the series was intended to demonstrate, by the choice of select examples, certain of the more significant obstacles that stand in the way of the diffusion of knowledge, techniques, or ideas, and it was hoped to demonstrate that a failure in the transmission of such cultural elements could not be held to establish the breakdown of the theory or historic fact of diffusion itself.

In the course of the study, one fundamental factor stands out, a factor which, like a shoal hidden under the high tide of argument, has caused the wreck of many a well-reasoned case. This factor is conservatism.

It was, we have seen, conservatism which determined or impeded the spread of the craft of metallurgy, and it was suggested that it was principally the scourge of war that encouraged its spread. It was conservatism in priestly circles that turned a blind eye to the earliest evolution of the written word, and progress in the form of commerce that stimulated it. It was poverty, the conservatism of human economics, that restricted the free passage of the wheel, and limitation of the scale of cultivation that denied to the peasant the benefits of the plough and the draught-animal. On the other hand, it was conservatism, the conservatism of religious concepts and of priestly and kingly hierarchies, that sowed the world with imperishable monuments of stone.

Conversely, the paper was designed as a warning to impulsive students of a technological turn of mind not to reject, in the field of any special study, the possibilities of exotic influence, simply on the score that their models had failed to make use of what are now understood to be essential and basic techniques.

The archaic civilisation was devoted, above all else, to the service of the gods. From the gods came all that was good, and to the gods it must be returned. In the gods lay man's hope of immortality, or, in times of flagging imagination, long life, health, and prosperity.

We have not attempted to establish with full supporting evidence the power of obscurantism in human affairs, because in some form or other it is omnipresent.

Prejudice of circumstantial origin has led peoples into extremes of self-mortification. How extraordinary of the Chinese to deny themselves the benefits of the basic animal diet—milk! But they had no choice: their mortal enemies, the nomads, largely subsisted on it.

Similarly, Mr. E. R. Leach has argued, in *Political Systems of Highland Burma,* which is a study of that lingually divided people, the Kachins, that stability of language is only to be found within a stable political system, dominated by a feudal hierarchy, where it becomes a status symbol: but that where there is overall political instability 'dialects change every few miles, almost from village to village', so that the unity of the village is preserved, while a bland and stony facade is presented to disreputable neighbours.

Nor do we desire to denigrate the virtues of conservatism, without which the advances made by civilisation could not have been consolidated. In the guise of superstition it is deplorable, and superstition itself creeps, like some serpent escaped from Eden, into every aspect of human life, including those ideas which are cast in the parts of progress. Let us beware of prejudices which combine expediency and morality. Once upon a time it was impious to apply steel to the hairs of the head and beard. It has frequently in history been impious to own property, but this does not mean that history could safely discard the property principle. At times man was the property of the gods, now he is the property of the state: the amalgam of practical advantage with morality (of a kind) renders both ideas liable to the charge of superstition. To offend either concept is, or was, conceived as both unpractical and 'unlucky', or in some way fore-fated, even if conformity can be seen to result in a falling off of the quality of human life, and of its fullest expression.

Thus the well-oiled expression 'historical destiny' epitomises the superstitious principle in both study and action, the fatalism that has always offered resistance to the vitality of ideas.